THE REGIONAL DISTRIBUTION OF FOREIGN MANUFACTURING INVESTMENT IN THE UK

The Regional Distribution of Foreign Manufacturing Investment in the UK

Stephen Hill
Lecturer in Business Economics
Cardiff Business School

and

Max Munday
Lecturer in Business Economics
Cardiff Business School

First published 1994 by
THE MACMILLAN PRESS LTD
Houndmills, Basingstoke, Hampshire RG21 2XS
and London
Companies and representatives
throughout the world

ISBN 0–333–58649–2

A catalogue record for this book is available
from the British Library.

Printed in Great Britain by
Ipswich Book Co Ltd
Ipswich, Suffolk

This book is dedicated to the memory of
Joyce Brown
Cardiff Business School Librarian, 1983–92

'Our work, as indeed our world, is the poorer
without you.'

Contents

List of Tables

xi

List of Figures

Preface

The announcement that a foreign manufacturing firm intends to locate in a UK region is usually looked upon in a favourable manner. Much store is set by the promise of new jobs in areas hit by structural decline, or perhaps by the guarantee of jobs safeguarded through a foreign takeover. With larger foreign investments the national and local press, together with development agency officials and local politicians, are quick to point to the positive factors that have influenced the location decision of the firm. Such factors as quality of the local labour force, easy access to markets and availability of practical and financial assistance are often quoted. Yet published comments are unlikely to manifest those factors that have really influenced the multinational firm. Why is it, for example, that Wales and Scotland have done so well in attracting new foreign manufacturing investment in the 1980s, whilst the South East, with its large market, physical resources and proximity to the EC, has attracted relatively small levels of new foreign manufacturing?

These questions interest us. We had both been involved in studies examining the record levels of foreign manufacturing investment in Wales. Moving away from the purely descriptive, we used econometric analysis to examine the success of Wales in attracting high shares of UK inward investment. Yet in doing this we were only scratching the surface. At the wider level we needed to understand what determined the UK distribution of foreign manufacturing investment, especially the location of new manufacturing investment. Why is this important? New foreign manufacturing investment, together with the shifting stock of existing investment, makes a significant contribution to the UK economy. At the regional level the contribution of foreign manufacturing can be even more significant, making up a large proportion of local employment and output. Indeed the attraction of multinational manufacturing capital has become a key element of regional policy. Some understanding of the determinants of the distribution of foreign manufacturing is clearly important if we are to consider the correspondence of the objectives of the multinational firm with the needs of the UK regions.

In this volume we consider the determinants of the regional distribution of foreign manufacturing in the UK. This analysis, as suggested above, is put in the wider context of the economic needs and development of the regions, and the stated objectives of policy. The central thesis of the volume is that foreign investors will seek in their regional location decision to minimise production costs, while being constrained by the need to gain access to adjacent markets. Our analysis deals with the distribution of foreign manufacturing in the UK, but we present some preliminary evidence that suggests that such an hypothesis may have equal validity if we consider the location of new investment throughout the EC. This is important because, in trying to attract new inward investment, the regions of the UK are competing against an enlarged EC, and indeed areas of eastern Europe.

It is hoped that this volume will help to provide a deeper insight into the changing geography of overseas investment in the UK, and the location decisions of the multinational firm.

STEPHEN HILL
MAX MUNDAY

Acknowledgements

Much of the research in this book would have been impossible without the provision of information and advice from the Invest in Britain Bureau of the Department of Trade and Industry, the Welsh Development Agency and Locate in Scotland. In addition we would like to thank colleagues at the Cardiff Business School who have either directly or indirectly aided us during our research, especially Professor Mick Silver, Christos Ioannidis, Jonathan Morris, Annette Roberts and Julie Keegan. Heather Rowlands and Karen Trigg provided valuable secretarial support and a store of patience. Finally our thanks go to the Aberconway library staff at the Cardiff Business School for their help in providing data and publications to support the research.

S. H.
M. M.

1 UK Trends in Foreign Direct Investment

1.1 INTRODUCTION

The purpose of this chapter is to place foreign direct investment (FDI) in its UK context. The initial section of the chapter provides a definition of foreign direct investment. The second section shows the importance of flows of FDI to the UK economy, whilst the third section goes on to highlight the success of the UK in attracting new foreign manufacturing investment during the eighties. The final section considers why it is necessary to study the UK regional distribution of foreign inward investment, and outlines the content of the following chapters.

1.2 WHAT IS FDI?

Simply defining what constitutes foreign direct investment causes a number of problems. FDI is differentiated from portfolio investment, in that FDI involves the ownership of assets by foreign persons for the purpose of controlling the use of those assets. Portfolio investment on the other hand is the acquisition of foreign securities by foreign persons without any control or management necessarily implied. The general definition of FDI thus poses some important questions. For example, what constitutes control and ownership? Graham and Krugman (1989) comment on the definitional problems by referring to American practice. The US Department of Commerce defines a foreign investment as direct where one foreign investor acquires a 10 per cent stake in an enterprise. However, a 10 per cent stake may give no element of control in an enterprise, whereas an efficiently coordinated group of shareholders with minority stakes may be able to gain a large

measure of effective control. Problems of definition also involve
the nationality of inwardly investing 'persons'. This may be
difficult where the 'person' is a multinational global enterprise,
since in many cases FDI is the outworking of the activities of multinational enterprise.

With these problems noted, the definition of FDI used in the
UK is derived from the OECD 'Benchmark Definition'. Here
direct investment is: 'investment that adds to, deducts from, or
acquires a lasting interest in an enterprise operating in an economy other than that of the investor, the purpose being to have an
effective voice in the management of the enterprise'. Where there
is no 'effective voice' an investment is classed as being of the
portfolio type. Once again there are problems in defining what is
meant by an 'effective voice'.

Foreign direct investment can take many forms including
greenfield investments, mergers and acquisitions, joint ventures,
together with both majority and minority involvement by foreign
persons in British firms. The commentary on FDI within the UK
outlined below describes FDI in terms of capital flows between
the parent company and its overseas affiliates. However, it is
important to note that FDI may not always involve a transfer of
capital where manufacturing is involved. Whilst FDI is a transfer
of production, capital flows are not always required because the
parent company could be free to raise finance in host economies
or on the international capital market. In this sense the movement
of capital across borders is not always a conditional consequence
of FDI. FDI is then a function of the spatial rearrangement of
multinational enterprise activities. It is this spatial redistribution
of production that has attracted theoretical, political and practical
interest.

1.3   FDI AND THE UK

The UK has historically been a major player among the world's
direct investors. During the 1970s and early 1980s the UK was

the worlds second largest outward direct investor by size of capital stock, behind the US. This position has now been altered by the growing importance of Japanese overseas investment but the UK remains an important source of outward direct investment, and an increasingly significant host to inward investment. Table 1.1. shows flows of both inward and outward direct investment for the period 1984 to 1990. Provisional figures for 1991 are also included.

Outward direct investment by UK firms has historically been of greater magnitude than inward direct investment by foreign

Table 1.1   Direct overseas investment, UK, 1984–91 (£m)

	1984	*1985*	*1986*	*1987*	*1988*	*1989*	*1990*	*1991*
ODI*	6 003	8 442	11 783	19 215	20 839	21 462	9 655	10 216
IDI**	(181)	4 507	5 837	9 449	12 008	18 556	18 593	12 045

Note: * outward direct investment; ** inward direct investment.

Source: Business Monitor MA4, *Overseas Transactions 1990*, CSO.

Table 1.2   Sources of inward direct investment, UK, 1990

	Investment (£m)	*% of total*
European Community	5 772	31.0
Other West European	2 152	11.6
North America	4 911	26.4
Australia	1 232	6.6
Japan	1 705	9.2
Remainder	2 821	15.1
Total	18 593	100.0

Note: Remainder includes rest of world and miscellaneous investment of £1362m.

Source: Business Monitor MA4, *Overseas Transactions 1990*, CSO.

firms. However during 1991 provisional figures suggest that direct investment abroad by UK firms totalled around £10.2 billion, and earnings by UK firms on their overseas assets were around £13.5 billion. The net book value of UK net direct investment overseas was nearly £130 billion. Inward direct investment in 1991 was just over £12 billion, and foreign firms earned £5.8bn on their stock of UK direct investments. The net book value of FDI in the UK was £127 billion. Outward direct investment thus adds substantially to the UK balance of payments.

Outward direct investment is mainly channelled to Western Europe and North America, and it is these sources which are also the main sources of inward investment as shown in Table 1.2.

1.4   FOREIGN MANUFACTURING INDUSTRY IN THE UK

Just over 20 per cent of direct inward investment during 1990 was classified to manufacturing (Business Monitor, 1992). The fortunes of foreign manufacturing industry in the UK during the 1980s have been subject to volatility as evidenced by the numbers employed within it. At 1979 there were just under 975 000 people employed by foreign manufacturers in the UK. By 1987 this figure had fallen to just under 625 000 before recovering to just over 775 000 by 1990. This latter figure represented around 16 per cent of UK manufacturing employment, and was distributed among 1443 separate enterprises. Some indication of the relative importance of foreign manufacturing to UK manufacturing as a whole is provided in Table 1.3.

Although foreign manufacturing enterprises make up a small percentage of the total number of UK manufacturing enterprises, they tend to be much larger as shown by their shares of employment, sales (over a quarter) and output.

In terms of the international sources of this manufacturing investment (Table 1.4) North America accounted for around 47 per cent of the individual enterprises, and over 58 per cent of total employment. Dependence on North America as a source of invest-

Table 1.3   Foreign manufacturing in the UK, 1990, key statistics

	Foreign manufacturing	As % UK manufacturing
Enterprises	1 443	1.1
Employment (000s)	775.1	16.1
Total sales/work done (£m)	79 991.6	25.2
Net output (£m)	31 115.7	22.4
GVA at factor cost (£m)	24 063.9	21.8
Total net cap. exp. (£m)	3 844.7	27.0

Source: Census of Production (1990) *Summary Tables PA 1002*, CSO.

Table 1.4   Foreign-owned manufacturing in the UK: 1990, enterprises, employment and net output

Source	Enterprises	Employment (000s)	Net output (£m)
USA	642 (44.5)	402.1 (51.9)	17 340.5 (55.7)
Canada	42 (2.9)	51.0 (6.6)	1 911.3 (6.1)
EC	391 (27.1)	154.8 (20.0)	5 378.4 (17.3)
Australia	38 (2.6)	20.9 (2.7)	1 021.5 (3.3)
Japan	104 (7.2)	40.9 (5.3)	1 758.0 (5.7)
Switzerland	80 (5.5)	45.1 (5.8)	1 632.5 (5.3)
Sweden	63 (4.4)	30.3 (3.9)	820.3 (2.6)
Remainder	83 (5.8)	30.1 (3.9)	1 253.2 (4.0)
Total	1 443 (100.0)	775.1 (100.0)	31 115.7 (100.0)

Source: Census of Production (1990) *Summary Tables PA1002*, CSO.

ment is falling. In 1979 North American firms provided nearly 75 per cent of foreign manufacturing employment and accounted for nearly 78 per cent of net output. However, between 1979 and 1990, employment in North American manufacturing in the UK fell by around 270 000 people. The EC accounts for 27 per cent of enterprises but only 20 per cent of employment. The largest contributors from the EC were Germany (Federal republic) and France, whose investments together accounted for just over 90 000 employees. Japan is becoming more prominent as a UK inward investor, but in 1990 Japanese manufacturing enterprises still employed just 5 per cent of the total workforce of foreign owned manufacturing, and accounted for around 6 per cent of net foreign manufacturing output. However, some indication of growth in investment from this source is provided by the fact that during 1990 alone, Japanese manufacturers accounted for nearly 9 per cent of net capital expenditure committed by foreign manufacturers. In spite of this growth from Japan, it is still North America that remains the dominant international source, which is further evidenced by North American enterprises' share of total foreign manufacturing sales and output (around 62 per cent).

Table 1.5   Foreign manufacturing by sector, 1990

Sector	SIC	Employment (000s)	Total sales/work done (£million) % total	
Mechanical engineering	32	110.1	8 396.7	(10.5)
Vehicles/parts	35	109.0	13 961.3	(17.5)
Electronics, etc.	34	95.4	6 983.1	(8.7)
Chemicals	25	97.1	12 203.9	(15.3)
Paper products, etc.	47	65.2	6 035.2	(7.5)
Food, drink, tobacco	41/42	73.3	12 098.2	(15.1)
Rubber/plastics	48	46.6	3 171.7	(4.0)
Metal manufacture	22	23.6	3 081.0	(3.9)
Other metal goods	31	34.6	2 411.3	(3.0)
Non-metallic mineral	24	19.3	1 281.9	(1.6)
Office machinery, etc.	33	29.9	6 385.6	(8.0)
Other sectors	N/A	70.9	3 978.0	(5.0)
Total all sectors		775.1	79 991.6	

Source: Census of Production (1990) *Summary Tables PA 1002*, CSO.

In terms of main industrial sectors (see Table 1.5), mechanical engineering is the largest group ranked by employees, however in terms of sales (and net output) the motor vehicle and chemical industry accounts for around 33 per cent of the total. During the 1980s employment in the two largest employing sectors has fallen considerably. Between 1981 and 1989 around 100 000 jobs were lost in the foreign mechanical engineering and motor vehicle industries. These sectors have however recovered over 20 000 jobs during 1990. The majority of the remaining sectors have maintained employment at or near to 1981 levels.

1.5   THE UK AS A LOCATION FOR NEW INWARD INVESTMENT

The UK is a very popular location for footloose international capital investment projects. Within the enlarged EC the UK has tended to attract the lion's share of incoming investment. This may appear unlikely given that the UK is on the edge of the EC with no history of fixed transportation links to Europe, and in addition a record of low industrial productivity and high inflation coupled in the 1970s with labour relations difficulties. Furthermore labour costs in the UK may be higher than those now extant in some regions of the enlarged EC.

But the UK has many factors in its favour. It is a large consumer market in itself, and incoming plants have the added bonus of tariff free access to the wider EC with a market of 400 million people. In historical terms the UK has held an open door to inward investors. From the Department of Trade and Industry down to local development agencies, there is a network in place that seeks to attract inward investment from foreign firms. At the government level foreign inward investment is perceived as a positive opportunity for the creation of jobs and trading opportunities, often in poorer regions of the economy (see Chapter 4). Whilst labour costs may not be as cheap as those in other peripheral EC areas, actual conditions of employment are favourable for the foreign investor. Trades union legislation during the 1980s coupled with general economic conditions have created an accommodating industrial relations climate. Many US and Japanese investors have been successful in arriving at single union deals and a measure of industrial relations harmony. In addition to these factors there is wide ranging financial assistance for investors locating in certain regions, and importantly no controls on currency movements and profit remittances to home economies. Finally the use of the English language has been shown by survey evidence to be a relevant factor in the location decisions of US and Japanese enterprise (Munday, 1990).

Due to some combination of the above factors, between 1951 and 1990, the UK attracted 38 per cent of US direct investment coming into the EC, and over a similar period nearly 40 per cent of Japanese direct investment (Invest in Britain Bureau, 1993).

Table 1.6   New projects and associated employment, 1980–92

Year	Projects	New jobs
1980	155	18 662
1981	133	16 417
1982	133	10 529
1983	236	15 546
1984	328	27 102
1985	375	25 584
1986	339	16 274
1987	325	21 651
1988	352	27 653
1989	327	30 756
1990	356	27 181
1991	332	22 714
1992	303	16 998
Total	3 694	276 977

Source: Invest in Britain Bureau.

Some indication of the magnitude of the UK success in attracting new inward investment projects and jobs comes from Invest in Britain Bureau data (Table 1.6).

Between 1980 and 1992 the IBB was notified of nearly 3700 new foreign projects (including acquisitions, joint ventures and expansions) expected to result in associated employment of over 275 000 people. Although these figures need cautious interpretation they represent a considerable achievement. These new jobs do not include those safeguarded by new projects such as acquisitions. The principal sources of these new projects and jobs are the US, Japan and Germany. Around 65 per cent of new projects (73 per cent of total jobs) during 1992/1993 came from these sources according to the Invest in Britain Bureau (Table 1.7). Although in historical terms the US has been the principal provider of foreign inward investment in manufacturing, the late eighties and early nineties have seen the EC and Japan becoming equally important

Table 1.7   National sources of reported foreign projects and associated jobs, 1992

Country of origin	Projects	Associated jobs: total
USA	126	23 070
Germany	51	16 032
Japan	21	2 036
France	14	1 956
Switzerland	15	1 032
Holland	10	1 564
Sweden	10	1 019
Rest of Europe	30	5 601
Rest of world	26	3 961
Totals	303	56 271

Note: Associated jobs is an estimate of long-term employment associated with the project at the time of announcement and includes safeguarded employment.

Source: Invest in Britain Bureau.

as sources of new investment, not least in the non-core regions of the UK.

1.6   THE REGIONAL DISTRIBUTION OF NEW FOREIGN INWARD INVESTMENT

Historically a high proportion of foreign direct investment has been present in the South Eastern corner of England. For example, in 1963 over 50 per cent of foreign owned manufacturing company employment in the UK was concentrated in the South East (Census of Production, 1990). The propensity for multinational enterprises to locate in core regions of advanced industrial economies was illustrated more generally by Blackbourne (1978). In 1968 he found that 50 per cent of US plants by number were in the South East of England, and that similar multinational enterprise propensities to locate in the core region had been noted in studies that examined Canada, the US and separate EC states.

However, the geography of overseas investment in the UK has changed rapidly. Since 1945 there has been a sustained shift of new foreign manufacturing activity away from the UK core region towards both the near and far periphery. In 1990 the South East accounted for only 30 per cent of foreign manufacturing employment and 35 per cent of net output. This trend has been noted in other developed economies. For example in the United States, McConnell (1980) found that during the 1970s foreign firms were preferring to locate away from the traditional US manufacturing heartland. The regional patterns of foreign investment in the US were fully investigated by Glickman and Woodward (1988) in evidence examined later in this volume.

In the UK context, the foreign industry shift to the periphery has been supported by active periods of regional policy. Even in 1991 regional preferential assistance to industry in the UK periphery remains substantial, despite real cuts in absolute levels during the eighties (see Chapter 4). The 'pull' of the regions has been reinforced by the sustained marketing efforts of regional development agencies. The 'pull' has also been reinforced by 'push' factors in certain periods including the need for industrial development certificates in non-assisted areas.

For UK regions inward investors provide employment and incomes. They may also be in a position to transfer new skills and technologies, as well as providing new opportunities for locally based enterprises. It has been recognised for some time that the movement of foreign firms to assisted areas may have different consequences than the movement of British firms. Yannopoulous and Dunning (1976) showed the possibility that foreign industry, by virtue of its size, technology, product, organisation and managerial practices, may have a differential impact on the regional development of industry.

While the changing geography of overseas investment in the UK has been widely acknowledged (Dicken and Lloyd, 1976; McDermott, 1977; Hill and Munday, 1992) there is very little empirically based research that examines the new and changing distribution of overseas investment. McDermott (1977), considering this changing geography, commented that only with a refined knowledge and understanding of the UK distribution of foreign inward investment is it possible to move further and explore the impact of overseas direct investment upon UK regions. Unless one knows something about the actual determinants that underlie foreign company location decisions in the UK, it is unlikely that one can fully assess the possible economic consequences of such investments. For example the regional impact of a plant may differ according to whether its location decision was totally influenced by cost variables (such as the availability of cheap labour and subsidies) or whether it entered a region to utilise specific skills and supply/physical infrastructure.

Investigation of the distribution of foreign investment is particularly relevant because the attraction of internationally mobile capital projects remains at the forefront of economic policy for the regions, and is associated with a high level of expenditure and effort. The role of multinational enterprise in the local economy also continues to be a topic of both political and academic debate.

A welter of academic studies have questioned the usefulness of multinational enterprise in aiding the UK regional problem (see Chapter 3), and there is limited evidence that development agencies are beginning to be more selective in those projects targeted.

Key concerns in the Celtic regions of the UK economy have been about the nature and quality of employment created by multinationals, together with the precise nature of operations performed. The growing importance of Japanese manufacturing enterprise in these areas has added fuel to the debate. What is obvious however, is that the level of debate would benefit from clear empirical evidence rather than the anecdotal and the assumed.

1.7   OBJECTIVES OF THIS VOLUME

It is the purpose of the present volume to examine empirically the determinants of the distribution of foreign direct investment within the UK, alongside the regional development implications of this distribution. In seeking to achieve these objectives the structure of the book as is follows.

Within Chapter 2 we will seek to show why it is that firms decide to invest abroad, and why it is that specific locations are chosen. The problem is first addressed through a brief review of the various contributions that have been made to the theory of the multinational enterprise and foreign direct investment. The chapter goes on to consider those locational characteristics that have been shown by both empirical and survey evidence to be important to multinational firms in their locational decision making. An appreciation of the relevant theory and evidence will aid the development of those hypotheses that can explain the regional distribution of inward investment in the UK.

Chapter 3 goes on to examine the post-war distribution of foreign manufacturing investment in the UK in terms of both employment and output. Attention is drawn to the gradual ongoing shift of foreign investment away from the core regions and towards the UK periphery. An index of relative regional performance is constructed, which identifies regions that have been most successful in attracting new foreign investors during the eighties and early nineties. The chapter concludes with a closer examination of the four most relatively successful UK regions. Both the level and nature of foreign owned company investment in these 'winning' regions is considered. This provides a link to the following chapter, which provides an evaluation of the economic needs of the UK regions, and some assessment of the extent to which investment from multinational enterprise can fulfil these needs. As previously noted the value of footloose international investment is increasingly debated, so in this chapter there is an exploration of the evidence of the MNE contribution. The case for government intervention, the role of development agencies and other institutions within the policy framework is also assessed within a European context.

Chapter 5 builds upon theoretical evidence to develop hypotheses that seek to explain the regional distribution of inward investment in the UK. The core thesis of this book is that foreign investors will in their location decisions seek to minimise their overall costs of production. This cost minimisation will be constrained by the need to ensure that they are adjacent to their key markets, whether these be national or European. Thus regional success in attracting new foreign investment will be determined by the extent to which regions possess the characteristics to enable inwardly investing firms to minimise their production costs whilst accessing product markets. An empirical model is developed, with both dependent and independent variables carefully explained. This model is then estimated and is shown to confirm these hypotheses.

In Chapter 6 this model is developed further. The model is reassessed to highlight and examine the success of certain regional blocs. The usefulness of the model in pointing to likely future regional success both in the UK and Europe is also investigated.

The final chapter brings together the strands of the analysis and their implications. Confirmation of the hypotheses developed in Chapter 5 has important policy implications. If the regional distribution of new foreign projects is determined by cost influencing variables and the desire for market access, then there are important consequences for future regional development, and the role of MNE capital in this future development. It is hoped and intended that the reader completing this volume will have gained a deeper understanding of what has influenced the changing geography of overseas investment in the UK, and will appreciate the developmental consequences of these changes.

References

Blackbourne, A. (1978), 'Multinational Enterprises and Regional Development: A Comment', *Regional Studies*, 12, 125–7.

Business Monitor MA4 (1992), *Overseas Transactions 1990*, Newport: CSO.

Census of Production (1990), *Summary Tables PA1002*, Newport: CSO.

Dicken, P. and Lloyd, P. (1976), 'Geographical Perspectives on US Investment in the UK', *Environment and Planning A*, 8, 685–705.

Glickman, N. and Woodward, D. (1988), 'The Location of FDI in the US: Patterns and Determinants', *International Regional Science Review*, 11.2, 137–54.

Graham, E. M. and Krugman, P. (1989), *Foreign Direct Investment in the US*, Washington: Institute of International Economics.

Hill, S. and Munday, M. (1992), 'The UK Regional Distribution of FDI: Analysis and Determinants', *Regional Studies*, 26.6, 535–44.

Invest in Britain Bureau (1993), *Annual Report*, London: Department of Trade and Industry.

McConnell, J. E. (1980), 'FDI in the US', *Annals of the Institute of American Geographers*, 70.2, 259–70.

McDermott, P. J. (1977), 'Overseas Investment and the Industrial Geography of the UK', *Area*, 9, 200–207.

Munday, M. (1990), *Japanese Manufacturing Investment in Wales*, Cardiff: University of Wales Press.

Yannopoulous, G. N. and Dunning, J. H. (1976), 'Multinational Enterprises and Regional Development: An Exploratory Paper', *Regional Studies*, 10.4, 389–99.

2 The Motivation for Foreign Direct Investment

2.1 INTRODUCTION

Before going on to examine the distribution of foreign direct investment in the UK there is a need to examine why FDI takes place, and what seems likely to determine its distribution and location. Foreign direct investment is typically the outworking of the activities of the multinational enterprise and so consideration of FDI must start with why firms become multinational. In this chapter the main developmental contributions to a theory of why enterprises engage in FDI are outlined. These theoretical contributions are provided as background to the development of hypotheses later in this volume to explain the regional distribution of FDI in the UK. The basic motivations for FDI by MNEs may provide clues as to why specific locations are chosen.

Whilst these core theoretical contributions cast some light on why final locations are chosen, they can say little about what determines the distribution of FDI within a nation. The second part of this chapter includes specific consideration of the locational characteristics of host nations and regions that may have influenced the distribution of FDI. This section will review both empirical and survey evidence that has sought to establish why MNEs choose some locations in preference to others. Once more this will provide evidence of those factors that have influenced the regional distribution of FDI in the UK.

Note that a detailed survey and critique of the theory of the multinational firm is beyond the scope of this volume. The interested reader is directed to Pitelis and Sugden (1991) for an up-to-date evaluation of theoretical developments concerning the transnational firm.

2.2   MULTINATIONAL ENTERPRISE: A DEFINITION?

As was the case with FDI, actually defining what constitutes a multinational enterprise is fraught with problems. Definition could derive from any one of the many MNE characteristics. For example, a definition could be based around size parameters and the percentage of company assets or profits gained from overseas sources. Another definition might concentrate upon the number of countries in which a firm has productive operations. Yet the complexity of the modern MNE, and the many ways in which it can actually control overseas production, can undermine even the most carefully constructed definition. In the following chapters a multinational enterprise is defined as a corporation which owns (in whole or in part), controls and manages income generating assets in more than one country (Hood and Young, 1979).

2.3   ORIGINS OF A THEORY?

Initial theories concerning FDI viewed the process as a transfer of capital from capital rich to capital poor states. Trade theory showed that capital moved in response to international differences in rates of return. However, the persistent growth of the MNE in the post war era, and the increasing dominance and complexity of the MNE as an institution, posed more and more problems for existing economic theory. This led to the development, starting in the 1960s, of a new body of theory which seeks to explain why MNEs engage in international production.

In a perfectly competitive environment, foreign direct investment by MNEs would not occur. In entering the host market the inward investor would bear significant extra costs not borne by the domestically based competition. In part then foreign direct investment is a function of imperfect markets. Early contributions to the theory of the MNE centred around attempts to explain the nature of the 'specific advantage' of the MNE that allowed them to overcome the additional costs of operating and competing abroad (Hymer, 1976; Kindleberger, 1969; Caves, 1971).

Firm specific 'ownership' advantages could derive from a number of sources. One possibility is technologically based advantages. These may be the result of patented and differentiated products, or perhaps of a new method of production. For example Japanese multinationals producing electronics products are famed for their use of manufacturing methods which result in efficiency, quality, and an accelerated flow of materials through the plant. Caves (1974) shows that the ability to differentiate the product can be a specific advantage. At the same time, successful product differentiation needs good general marketing skills and may include the ability to brand goods. Other sources of specific advantage include favoured access to sources of finance, product markets, raw materials, and managerial/entrepreneurial skills. In the case of the latter some writers have suggested that foreign direct investment is the result of slack managerial resources. The firm will become multinational to utilise the whole of its managerial talent, particularly where slack talent exists in production and marketing areas (Caves, 1971).

Other advantages for the MNE may come as a result of oligopolistic market structures. The size of the firm may have a significant influence on its ability to innovate, conduct research and development, to fully exploit patents and to successfully differentiate products. Plant economies of scale, extant in oligopoly, may also be a source of specific advantage. Where multi-plant operations in the parent economy do not secure the full possible cost advantage, additional plants could be placed overseas until the scope of economies are exhausted.

Whilst the 'specific advantage' approach may show where the strength of the MNE lies, it does not in itself constitute a general theory of the MNE. For example, it says little about why the MNE, in possession of these advantages, does not exploit them through the process of exporting, or where this is not possible, through a process of licensing.

2.4   INTERNALISATION APPROACHES

In attempting to answer these problems theorists returned to the ideas of Coase (1937). Coase, in explaining the genesis of the firm, suggested that some transactions would be carried out within the business firm rather than by the market, due to the high transactions costs of some market operations.

Where the market fails, internalising market operations within the firm can offer several advantages. Where, for example, there is a failure in the market for final goods then internalisation may result in a reduction of the costs associated with market transactions. Where there is failure in the market for inputs then internalisation can lead to avoidance of costs associated with enforcing property rights, and the control of crucial supplies. Internalisation may allow the monopolistic firm to practise price discrimination and product differentiation (for example, in maintaining product quality).

Internalisation advantages can be used to explain why a multinational enterprise may prefer direct investment to licensing the overseas production of its goods. A licensing transaction involves costs in setting a price, defining mutual obligations and in enforcing agreements. Faced with such additional transaction costs the multinational firm might organise the transaction internally, that is, create a subsidiary abroad.

Buckley and Casson (1991) argued that the continued growth and development of MNE's during the twentieth century was influenced by the costs and benefits of internalising markets. Up until 1945 the main pressure for internalisation was the need of large firms to regulate future supplies of raw materials. Post 1945, the key force changed to the need of large firms to diffuse technical and marketing knowledge in a manner that maintained their proprietary rights (Buckley and Casson, 1991). An MNE is created wherever markets are internalised across national borders. Buckley and Casson believed that the internalisation of the market for knowledge in particular would cause a high degree of multinationality. Knowledge is a public good which can be easily transmitted across borders, and the full exploitation of knowledge requires internalisation achieved by a network of international plants.

During the 1980s, such transactions costs approaches have become the central explanation for the existence and growth of the MNE (Kay, 1983). Further commentary on recent advances in transactions costs approaches can be found in Cantwell (1991).

2.5   THE ECLECTIC PARADIGM

Dunning's 'Eclectic Paradigm' uses concepts from both the 'specific advantage' and internalisation approaches to explain the level and patterns of the firm or nations foreign investment activities. To explain the extent and level of international production, Dunning shows that three major factors will be important. Firstly, the competitive advantages that foreign firms have over the domestically based enterprises. These net ownership advantages' will compensate the foreign firm for the disadvantages faced when operating in a foreign environment. The nature of such advantages was considered earlier in this chapter. In Dunning's (1986) study of Japanese manufacturing investment in the UK, the ownership advantages possessed by Japanese multinationals included:

i.   A flexible manufacturing and working system.
ii.   The ability to foster both manager and worker commitment.
iii. Favoured access to supplies of intermediate goods.

The second aspect of the paradigm is the extent to which the firm in possession of these net ownership advantages finds it more profitable to internalise these advantages and hence to extract the maximum rent from them than available alternatives. For example FDI may be more profitable than licensing because of high transactions costs. In his study of Japanese manufacturing investment, Dunning (1986) suggests that FDI was preferred to licensing because, with direct investment, Japanese electronic firms could maintain quality standards by controlling the way that resources were used. The final element of the paradigm is that it must be more profitable for the firm to locate production within the host economy rather than to export directly to it.

Dunning (1991) states that 'the eclectic paradigm is to be regarded more as a framework for analysing the determinants of international production than a predictive theory of the multinational firm'. Using the eclectic paradigm (OLI: Ownership–Location–Internalisation) competitive advantage is first attributed to firms and nations which will then effect the extent and form of the firms international involvement.

Dunning (1979) posits that there are links between the net ownership advantages possessed by firms and the specific characteristics of nations. A nation having high per capita incomes, developed education and training facilities, a substantial skills base, high levels of R and D incentives and an efficient capital market might be classified as entrepreneurially competitive. These national advantages are internalised within the firm as intangible assets. With these assets the firm does not have to limit production to one nation, but may have the incentive to locate production overseas to access markets, reduce transportation costs, or perhaps to take advantage of special conditions and factor costs in the host country. The combination of a nations entrepreneurial competitiveness and locational attractiveness will thus determine mutual investment flows. For example a country such as the US is both entrepreurially competitive and locationally attractive, and can then be expected to be characterised by high levels of both inward and outward investment. Developing nations are unlikely to be entrepreurially competitive, but may be locationally attractive due to low factor costs. Then inward direct investment would be relatively high compared to outward direct investment.

The eclectic paradigm has attracted a great deal of attention and criticism, but Dunning (1991) shows that at least some of the criticism is due to the misconception of the eclectic paradigm as a theory of international production rather than a framework of analysis.

2.6   PRODUCT LIFE CYCLE APPROACHES

One theoretical approach to foreign direct investment has developed around the concept of the product life cycle. Vernon (1971) used the concept of the product life cycle to explain US investment into Western Europe in the postwar period. Four distinct stages in the sales life of a product can be identified. In the introductory stage, products may still be in semi-development, design is subject to change, production costs are high and margins low because of the need to cover high fixed development costs. During this stage the number of competitors will be few, and the product highly differentiated. During the growth stage product quality improves, mass production begins, an element of standardisation allows greater product reliability and increased margins. As the product becomes mature, standardisation is complete, and product differentiation with competing products is reduced. Competitive pressure increases and prices fall, but margins remain acceptable because of high volumes. During the decline stage competition among producers of the standardised product becomes intense. Margins fall, and the industry becomes characterised by over-capacity. In the decline stage firms may exit the market or redeploy resources.

The product cycle thesis relates these stages in the life cycle to the international location decision made by the firm, and to the choice between exporting and direct investment. As noted earlier, Vernon (1971) illustrated this approach with reference to the influx of US investment into Western Europe during the post war era. The development and introduction of new products was fuelled by effective demand. In the mid-twentieth century the US economy was characterised by high per capita incomes, with high incentives for US producers to manufacture new goods. The firms production was concentrated in the US during the introductory and initial growth stages because of the need to redesign, develop and market the product. This stage required highly skilled production and extensive functional communication. As competitors were few and the product highly differentiated at the genesis stage, cost considerations were marginalised. Hence there was a strong motive to produce in the home market.

With maturity products become standardised, and price competition becomes more important, as does production cost. Increased domestic competition and market expansion may highlight opportunities in overseas markets. These will be served via exports until cost considerations make it economic for direct investment. Initially foreign production takes place in a market where incomes are high but factor costs low. This characterised Western Europe during the 1950s and 1960s. With full standardisation and intense competition during the decline stage, production costs become all important. During this stage production is switched to the least cost source of supply (typically the developing economies).

Whilst Vernon's product cycle theory can explain the post-war expansion of US industry it is essentially time-bounded. It fails to explain US MNE production of non-standard products in Western Europe, and the process whereby during the introductory stage products are differentiated and developed for the needs of separate market blocs. Furthermore, the theory fails to explain trends in the global localisation of functions other than production.

Vernon (1974) modified the product cycle model to account for oligopolistic behaviour. Under this modified analysis, the firm invests abroad during the mature stage of the cycle so as to minimise risk, and to avoid extensive price competition. As economies of scale constitute an effective entry barrier during the mature phase, existing producers become very sensitive to the strategic movements of one another. Within this scenario, FDI may be a reaction to the foreign investment decision of competitors. The end result of both moves and countermoves by the oligopolists is stability in world market shares, which is partly achieved as each seeks to produce in the others national markets.

FDI as a result of oligopolistic interaction and rivalry was also investigated by Knickerbocker (1973), with a recent appreciation of the role of oligopolistic rivalry in multinational firm behaviour undertaken by Graham (1991).

2.7   NEW INTERNATIONAL DIVISION OF LABOUR

The New International Division of Labour Model (NIDLM) emphasises that FDI results from the attempts of global enterprise to locate its functions in different geographical areas to maximise net income (Frobel *et al.*, 1980; Casson, 1986; Schoenberger, 1988). In this context the multinational enterprise might separate its functions in the following manner;

1.   Key control and strategic functions are retained within the home economy.
2.   Distribution, sales, marketing and design functions are placed within target markets.
3.   Production is located at a least-cost supply point.

The pattern may be expected to vary from firm to firm. For example, research on new products may remain in the home economy if scale considerations are important. Also in a practical sense production will have to be placed within a target market when tariff barriers are significant, or where the availability of skilled manufacturing personnel is a requirement. Thus in reality, the drive to locate in least cost production areas may be constrained. Importantly however, the model shows that market access will be a consideration in the final location decision. The model may also go some way to explaining concentrations of foreign 'branch plants' in peripheral regions of developed economies (that is least-cost locations with access to target markets), and thus fuel debate about the regional development impact of plants with a limited range of functional ability and purpose.

2.8   SPECIFIC LOCATION CHARACTERISTICS AND FDI

The above review of contributions to the theory of FDI sheds some light on why it is, at the macro level at least, that some nations are chosen in preference to others as locations for the direct investment of MNEs. To the above approaches (that is eclectic paradigm, product cycle, and new international division of labour) could be added other approaches that may explain the preference for some national locations over others. For example, Kojima (1973) explained the overseas development of Japanese industry in terms of changing comparative advantages in factor endowments between nations. Empirically based studies have also attempted to show what determines FDI flows to nations. For example Lunn (1980), Scaperlanda and Balough (1983), together with Culem (1988) showed that bilateral FDI flows between the US and Europe were influenced by the size of host market, economic growth in the host market and the presence of tariff barriers. Arpan and Ricks (1975), examining FDI flowing into the US from the EC, concluded that this investment was an oligopolistic response to the direct investments of US firms into Europe. FDI in the US allowed European firms to protect American markets in the face of protectionism, and to gain access to US technology. Vernon (1971) examining European and Japanese investment in the US, largely concurred with these findings but added that tariff *and* non-tariff barriers were important, as were rising transport costs. Thus, in the bulk of surveys, market access and market growth factors appear to be important determinants of international FDI flows.

Whilst empirical investigation has provided some indication of the likely determinants and direction of flows of FDI to national locations, far less is known about why one location within a host nation is chosen in preference to another by foreign investors. In other words the empirically based evidence of the determinants of the sub-national geography of overseas investment is sparse.

Studies of the locational characteristics attractive to foreign investors have followed two principle paths. Survey based evidence has often been gleaned from the investors themselves, through both questionnaire and interview. Unfortunately such techniques only provide an indication of the final site characteristics that were important to incoming firms. There are two central reasons for this. Firstly, survey respondents are not always those who have been involved in the actual siting decision process. Secondly, true location attractions may not be divulged for reasons of good public relations. For example, empirically based evidence examining the attractiveness of Wales to inward investors highlights the importance of regional preferential assistance and labour costs, whilst such cost considerations rarely come out in questionnaire based survey work (Munday, 1990; Hill and Munday, 1991; Arthur D. Little, 1986). In assessing general survey evidence from the UK, Hood and Young (1983) concluded that both market size and incentives levels were important in explaining the distribution of FDI across the UK.

Empirical investigation of the regional characteristics attractive to foreign investors has been limited. However, in the US regression methods have been used in a small number of cases to seek to establish those regional factors that influence foreign investors. Little (1978) regressed US state characteristics on state shares of foreign investment relative to shares of domestic manufacturing. Little found that foreign investors were more sensitive than US investors to wage differentials and port infrastructure.

McConnell (1980) examined the extent to which the location pattern of foreign subsidiaries in the US corresponded to the changing spatial distribution of domestic firms. As part of his analysis he suggested that state shares of FDI increased as (among other things),:

a. the number of manufacturing units with more than 20 employees per capita increased,
b. as the states urban population increased relative to total population, and as states population per square mile increased,
c. as the state social well-being index declined,
d. if the state was within the traditional manufacturing belt,
e. as direct general expenditure per capita of state and local government increased, and
f. as federal aid per capita to state and local government decreases.

This analysis hints at a whole host of characteristics, not all as expected. McConnell also found that the variables that were expected to affect shifts in domestic manufacturing, that is personal/corporate taxes, climate, labour cost and trades union activity did *not* affect FDI. Thus in 1976 foreign firms in the US still preferred traditional locations, and were only just beginning to respond to the location decisions made by domestic firms in the 1960s and early 1970s to site facilities outside the traditional manufacturing heartlands.

Glickman and Woodward (1988) investigated the location pattern of foreign owned companies in the US, with regression results suggesting that the location of foreign owned property, plant and equipment could be largely explained by variables representing the cost of energy, infrastructure availability and labour climate, the latter variable incorporating industrial relations records and wages. Bagchi-Sen and Wheeler (1989), examined the spatial distribution of FDI among US metropolitan areas for the years 1974–78 and 1979–83. They tested the importance of population size (representing the growth of a metropolitan centre) and population growth (representing regional dynamics), together with per capita purchasing power, in determining levels of foreign investment. Each variable was found to be empirically significant.

Evidence from the UK has been equally limited. Dunning and Norman (1979) applied the eclectic model to examine the determinants of MNE office location in the UK. The factors that they noted as important in these location decisions included market size, resource availability, and good communications networks. Hill and Munday (1991) examined the success of Wales in attracting high levels of new inward investment during the 1980s. They found that the UK/Wales earnings differential was the most important determining factor in explaining high Welsh levels and UK shares of foreign investment and associated jobs. High relative levels of regional preferential assistance and infrastructure spending also contributed to the success of Wales.

In conclusion, it is necessary to concur with the analysis of Glickman and Woodward (1988), who in reviewing the evidence on spatial patterns of foreign investment in the US, stated:

The survey evidence indicates that locational factors describing regional production conditions appear far more important to foreign managers than state and local incentives. Consistently, the influence of markets, transportation facilities, and labour variables has emerged.

Analysis of those factors that affect the subnational distribution of FDI will be extended in Chapter 5. The next chapter considers the distribution of FDI within the UK.

References

Arpan, J. and Ricks, D. A. (1975), *Directory of Foreign Manufacturers in the US*, Atlanta: School of Business Administration, Georgia State University.

Arthur, D. Little Limited (1986), *The Japanese Experience in Wales*, Cardiff: Wales Investment Location.

Bagchi-Sen, S. and Wheeler, J. O. (1989), 'A Spatial and Temporal Model of FDI in the US', *Economic Geography*, 65.2, 113–129.

Buckley, P. J. and Casson, M. (1991), *The Future of the Multinational Enterprise*, London: Macmillan (1st edn 1976).

Cantwell, J. (1991), 'A Survey of Theories of International Production', Chapter 2 in C. N. Pitelis and R. Sugden (eds), *The Nature of the Transnational Firm*, London: Routledge.

Casson, M. (1986), *Multinationals and World Trade*, London: Allen & Unwin.

Caves, R. E. (1971), 'International Corporations: The Industrial Economics of Foreign Investment', *Economica*, 28, 1–27.

Caves, R. E. (1974), 'Causes of Direct Investment: Foreign Firms Shares in Canadian and UK Manufacturing Industries', *Review of Economics and Statistics*, 56, 272–293.

Coase, R. H. (1937), 'The Nature of the Firm', *Economica*, 4, 386–405.

Culem, C. (1988), 'The Locational Determinants of Direct Investment among Industrialised Countries', *European Economic Review*, 32, 885–904.

Dunning, J. H. (1979), 'Explaining Changing Patterns of International Production: In Defence of the Eclectic Theory', *Oxford Bulletin of Economics and Statistics*, 41.4, 269–295.

Dunning, J. H. (1986), *Japanese Participation in British Industry*, London: Croom Helm.

Dunning, J. H. (1991), 'The Eclectic Paradigm of International Production', Chapter 5 in C. N. Pitelis and R. Sugden (eds), *The Nature of the Transnational Firm*, London: Routledge.

Dunning, J. H. and Norman, G. (1979), *Factors Influencing the Location of Offices of Multinational Enterprises*, London: Location of Offices Bureau and Economists Advisory Group Limited.

Frobel, F, Heinrichs, J. and Kreye, O. (1980), *The New International Division of Labour*, Cambridge: Cambridge University Press.

Glickman, N. and Woodward, D. (1988), 'The Location of FDI in the US: Patterns and Determinants', *International Regional Science Review*, 11.2, 137–154.

Graham, E. M. (1991), 'Strategic Management and Transnational Firm Behaviour', Chapter 7 in C. N. Pitelis and R. Sugden (eds), *The Nature of the Transnational Firm*, London: Routledge.

Hill, S. and Munday, M. (1991), 'The Determinants of Inward Investment: A Welsh Analysis', *Applied Economics*, 23, 1761–9.

Hood, N. and Young, S. (1979), *The Economics of Multinational Enterprise*, London: Longman.

Hood, N. and Young, S. (1983), *Multinational Investment Strategies in the British Isles*, London: HMSO.

Hymer, S. (1976), *International Operations of National Firms: A Study of Foreign Direct Investment*, Cambridge, Mass.: MIT Press.

Kay, N. M. (1983), 'Multinational Enterprise: A review article', *Scottish Journal of Political Economy*, 30, 304–312.

Kindleberger, C. P. (1969), *American Business Abroad: Six Lectures on Direct Investment*, New Haven, Conn.: Yale University Press.

Knickerbocker, F. T. (1973), *Oligopolistic Reaction and the Multinational Enterprise*, Cambridge, Mass: Harvard University Press.

Kojima, K. (1973), 'A Macroeconomic Approach to FDI', *Hitotsubashi Journal of Economics*, 14.1, 1–21.

Little, J. S. (1978), 'Locational Decisions of Foreign Direct Investors in the US', *New England Economic Review*, July/August, 43–63.

Lunn, J. (1980), 'Determinants of US Direct Investment in the EEC', *European Economic Review*, January, 93–101.

McConnell, J. E. (1980), 'FDI in the US', *Annals of the Institute of American Geographers*, 70.2, 259–270.

Munday, M. (1990), *Japanese Manufacturing Investment in Wales*, Cardiff: University of Wales Press.

Pitelis, C. N. and Sugden, R. (eds) (1991), *The Nature of the Transnational Firm*, London: Routledge.

Scaperlanda, A. E. and Balough, R. S. (1983), 'Determinants of US Direct Investment in the EEC', *European Economic Review*, May, 381–390.

Schoenberger, E. (1988), 'Multinational Corporations and the New International Division of Labour: A Critical Approach', *International Regional Science Review*, 11.2, 105–119.

Vernon, R. (1971), *Sovereignty at Bay*, New York: Basic Books.

Vernon, R. (1974), 'The Location of Economic Activity', in J. H. Dunning (ed.) *Economic Analysis and the Multinational Enterprise*, London: Allen & Unwin.

3 The Regional Distribution of Foreign Direct Investment in the UK

3.1 INTRODUCTION

In Chapter 1 it was shown that foreign manufacturing enterprises employed just over 775 000 people in the UK economy in 1990, although employment within foreign owned manufacturing industry had fallen by nearly a quarter of a million in the decade to 1989 (IDS, 1990). This reflected a fall in the employment provided by US subsidiaries in the UK which has more than offset any growth in manufacturing employment provided by investments from the EC and Far East. In 1989 employment within foreign owned manufacturing industry in the UK was at its lowest levels since the early 1970s. Employment levels in foreign manufacturing however recovered substantially (by around 50 000) in 1990.

As absolute employment levels within the foreign owned manufacturing base have changed, so too has the regional distribution of employment provided, so that although the absolute level of foreign manufacturing employment in 1990 was similar to its 1971 level, the distribution of this employment across the standard regions was very different.

This change in the distribution of employment reflects the changes in the distribution of foreign investment which are the subject matter of this chapter. In the first section there is an examination of the movement of overseas direct investment away from the core region of the South East towards the periphal regions of the UK. For the 1980s in particular there is evidence of both shifts in overseas company employment and output across

29

regions, together with consideration of regional levels of foreign investment on the basis of Census of Production data.

The second part of the chapter uses data from the Invest in Britain Bureau of the Department of Trade and Industry to identify those mainland UK standard regions that have been most successful in attracting new foreign inward investment during the 1980s. This section will develop a method of measuring relative regional success in attracting new inward investment from overseas sources. Such a measure allows examination of why some regions are more successful than others in attracting overseas investment. The third section of the chapter looks more closely at the experience of the most successful standard regions, with the final section providing conclusions.

3.2   THE CHANGING DISTRIBUTION OF FOREIGN MANUFACTURING EMPLOYMENT AND INVESTMENT IN THE UK

Prior to 1945 overseas controlled manufacturing industry was largely concentrated in the South East corner of England. Since the war the distribution of this industry has become far more widespread. Evidence of this changing distribution can be observed from reference to the changing distribution of foreign manufacturing employment across UK regions (Table 3.1).

McDermott (1977), commenting upon shifts in foreign manufacturing employment between 1963 and 1971, noted that a general shift to the periphery could not be disputed. Comparison of the 1971 and 1990 regional shares of foreign manufacturing employment consolidates this conclusion. Between 1971 and 1990, the South East regions share of foreign manufacturing employment fell from 41 per cent to 28 per cent, or a loss of around 85 000 jobs (a fall of 28 per cent). Most of the mainland regions saw their shares of foreign manufacturing employment increase during the period, with the shares of two regions (North West and Scotland), falling only steadily in spite of being hit by

Table 3.1 The distribution of foreign manufacturing employment in the UK

Region	\multicolumn{8}{c}{Employment 000s (and as % UK)}							
	\multicolumn{2}{c}{1963}	\multicolumn{2}{c}{1971}	\multicolumn{2}{c}{1981}	\multicolumn{2}{c}{1990}
Northern	8.5	(1.6)	24.4	(3.3)	42.4	(4.9)	49.3	(6.4)
Yorks/ Humber	20.6	(3.8)	24.6	(3.3)	49.9	(5.8)	56.1	(7.2)
East Mids.	18.3	(3.4)	26.4	(3.5)	41.3	(4.8)	45.2	(5.8)
East Ang.	17.3	(3.2)	30.4	(4.1)	36.5	(4.3)	33.9	(4.4)
South East	277.9	(51.4)	305.2	(41.1)	310.7	(36.2)	220.3	(28.4)
South West	4.1	(0.8)	19.4	(2.6)	42.8	(5.0)	39.7	(5.1)
West Mids.	46.1	(8.5)	67.0	(9.0)	68.0	(7.9)	89.8	(11.6)
North West	70.5	(13.1)	97.9	(13.2)	115.0	(13.4)	91.7	(11.8)
Wales	24.0	(4.4)	35.5	(4.8)	45.4	(5.3)	49.3	(6.4)
Scotland	45.7	(8.5)	82.4	(11.1)	81.5	(9.5)	77.3	(10.0)
North Ire.	7.3	(1.3)	29.4	(4.0)	24.8	(2.9)	22.3	(2.9)
UK	540.3	(100.0)	742.7	(100.0)	858.1	(100.0)	775.1	(100.0)

Source: Census of Production, *Summary Tables PA 1002*, CSO, various.

large losses in the foreign automotive sector. The Northern and Yorkshire/Humberside regions have done particularly well during the 1970s and 1980s, witnessing more than a doubling of foreign manufacturing employment.

Between 1979 and 1987 employment in foreign manufacturing fell by 36 per cent (from 974 000 to 625 000), whilst between 1987 and 1990 this employment recovered by 150 000. The largest contraction in employment was in the South East during the early to mid-1980s, and this has added to the further redistribution of foreign manufacturing employment across the UK. These latter movements are summarised in Table 3.2, which examines regional gains and losses in foreign manufacturing employment between 1981 and 1990. Expected manufacturing employment

Table 3.2   The redistribution of foreign manufacturing employment, 1981–90

| Region | Employment in thousands | | | |
	Actual 81	Actual 90	Expected 1990 (9.7% reduction)	Deviation (000s)
Northern	42.4	49.3	38.3	+11.0
Yorks/Humber	49.9	56.1	45.1	+11.0
East Midlands	41.3	45.2	37.3	+7.9
East Anglia	36.5	33.9	33.0	+0.9
South East	310.7	220.3	280.7	−60.4
South West	42.8	39.7	38.7	+1.0
West Midlands	68.0	89.8	61.4	+28.4
North West	115.0	91.7	103.9	−12.2
Wales	45.4	49.3	41.0	+ 8.3
Scotland	81.5	77.3	73.6	+ 3.7
Northern Ireland	24.8	22.3	22.4	−0.1
United Kingdom	858.1	775.1	775.1	

Source: Census of Production, *Summary Tables PA 1002*, CSO, various.

for the regions has been estimated on the basis that numbers employed within overseas controlled subsidiaries contracted at the same rate as for the UK as a whole over the period, that is, 9.7 per cent.

Table 3.2 shows that mainland regions (with the exception of the South East and North West) have maintained employment at a fairly high level in spite of national reductions in foreign manufacturing employment. Once again then, the most recent evidence suggests a continuing redistribution of investment towards the periphery of the UK. Watts (1982) showed that during the 1970s the spatial distribution of foreign firms favoured the far rather than the near periphal regions. Evidence from Table 3.2 suggests that both the East and West Midlands (the near periphery) have fared well during the 1980s, although it is noted that the Table 3.2 tells us very little about a regions performance in attracting new inward investment.

Turning to a comparison of foreign manufacturing in UK regions based on Census of Production data, first note that some regions are clearly more dependent upon foreign investors for manufacturing employment than others (Table 3.3).

According to Census of Production data, in 1990 only 9 per cent of manufacturing employment in the East Midlands was

Table 3.3   The relative regional importance of foreign manufacturing industry employment, 1990

Region	Foreign manufacturing employment as % of regional manufacturing employment	Foreign manufacturing employment as % of total regional employment	Location quotient*
Northern	17.3	4.4	1.32
Yorks/Humber	11.6	3.1	0.91
East Midlands	9.1	2.8	0.85
East Anglia	19.4	4.3	1.28
South East	17.2	2.8	0.83
South West	10.6	2.2	0.67
West Midlands	13.8	4.3	1.28
North West	13.5	3.7	1.10
Wales	19.7	4.9	1.46
Scotland	18.3	3.9	1.16
N.Ireland	21.4	4.2	1.27
UK average	14.9	3.3	N/A

Note: *Location quotient is defined as the ratio of regional share of foreign owned employment to regional share of all employment.

Source: Census of Production, *Summary Tables PA 1002*, CSO, various.

attributable to foreign investors, whilst in Wales, Scotland, Northern Ireland and East Anglia, around 1 in 5 manufacturing jobs were within foreign owned enterprises. During the 1980s, the majority of regions with substantial Assisted Areas saw their proportion of UK foreign manufacturing employment increase. This movement was most notable in the Northern region, which saw its share of UK foreign owned manufacturing employment leap from 12.5 per cent to 17.3 per cent between 1981 and 1990. The West Midlands, on the same basis, saw its share increase from 8.3 per cent to 13.8 per cent over the same period.

Something of the relative importance of foreign manufacturing to UK regions is shown by the Location Quotient (LQ) which is here defined as the ratio of regional share of UK foreign manufacturing employment to regional share of all employment. For example if a region had 10 per cent of UK foreign manufacturing employment, but only 5 per cent of UK total employment it would have an LQ of 2. Table 3.3. provides LQ data for 1990. The highest LQs in 1990 were found in those regions with substantial Assisted Areas. East Anglia is the one exception. Wales has the highest location quotient (1.46), and this chapter will later confirm that Wales has succeeded in attracting record levels of inward foreign investment through the 1980s and early 1990s.

The distribution of foreign firm employment is also reflected in regional shares of foreign manufacturing output (Table 3.4). With movements away from the core regions during the 1980s, most of the near and far periphery have seen their share of foreign manufacturing output increase. In spite of this, in 1990, 33 per cent of foreign manufacturing output remained in the South East (and 31 per cent of gross value added). During 1990, output per employee was greatest in the South East of England, the North West and Scotland, and lowest in Yorkshire/Humberside. Although not shown in the table, gross value added displays a similar pattern.

Table 3.4. also provides information on net capital expenditure per employee. In 1990 net capital expenditure per employee was highest in Wales followed by the North West. These differences are reflected in data for other years during the 1980s. Table 3.5

Table 3.4   The distribution of foreign manufacturing output and output/net capital expenditure per employee

| | *Foreign manufacturing company* | | | |
| | *Distn of output (%)* | | *Output per* | *Net capital spend* |
	1981	*1990*	*employee,* *1990 (£)*	*per employee,* *1990 (£)*
North	4.8	6.2	39 398	6 734
Yorks/Humber	4.5	5.5	30 324	3 663
East Mids.	5.2	5.4	37 075	3 434
East Anglia	3.9	4.1	37 625	4 227
South East	39.6	32.7	46 255	4 158
South West	4.2	4.1	31 839	3 446
West Mids.	6.3	9.1	31 388	2 788
North West	13.3	13.1	44 471	7 011
Wales	5.3	6.4	40 034	9 941
Scotland	10.0	10.8	43 473	5 653
North Ireland	2.7	2.6	36 839	6 067
Total	£13 099.0m	£31 115.0m		

Source: Census of Production, *Summary Tables PA 1002*, CSO, various.

Table 3.5   Average annual net capital expenditure per employee, 1981, 1983–5, 1987–9 (1985 prices)

	£		£
North	4 148	West Midlands	1 753
Yorks/Humber	2 535	North West	3 733
East Midlands	2 253	Wales	5 352
East Anglia	2 321	Scotland	3 988
South East	2 989	Northern Ireland	3 698
South West	2 325		

Source: Census of Production, *Summary Tables PA 1002*, CSO, various.

shows the average annual net capital expenditure per employee at 1985 prices for seven years of the 1980s. This gives some indication of the capital intensity of new investments entering the regions. Although the data does not cover 1982 and 1986, it does show that the Celtic regions together with the North West and North have had far greater new investment per employee than other regions.

In conclusion, evidence from the Census of Production data indicates a sustained shift in investment away from the core region towards both the far and near periphery regions. FOC manufacturing employment is becoming more concentrated in regions benefiting from Assisted Area status. However, the analysis to date leaves unanswered questions as to which of the regions have been most successful in attracting new inward investment from overseas.

3.3   WHO ARE THE WINNING REGIONS?

Regional competition to host new foreign investment has become intense during the 1980s. Nowhere was this more evident than in inter-regional competition to host the prestigious Nissan and Toyota investments. The previous section suggested that peripheral regions of the UK have benefited from the redistribution of foreign investment away from the South East. However, the preceding analysis, relying as it does on historical Census of Production data, tells us little about those regions who have performed best in attracting new foreign investment. Any investigation which tries to locate the best performing regions immediately comes to a difficult hurdle in actually measuring what constitutes success. The analysis of this section measures success in terms of numbers of new projects and associated new jobs. It is readily recognised that those regions that succeed in attracting the highest numbers of new jobs and projects may not necessarily be winners in the normal sense of the word. The quality of inward manufacturing investment is all important. Unfortunately, quantitatively measuring the intrinsic quality of inward investment is an all but impossible exercise. Indeed, it is difficult enough even to locate accurate statistics on new foreign projects and jobs going to the standard regions of the UK.

With the above qualification noted, this section examines data provided by the Invest in Britain Bureau (IBB) of the Department of Trade and Industry. The IBB compiles information on new projects coming to UK regions (including greenfield ventures, joint ventures, expansions, and acquisitions) together with both newly created and safeguarded jobs. IBB data refers to announced new projects, together with the associated number of new jobs connected with projects. Very often this represents a three year projection of connected employment, often estimated by the investors themselves. Then one problem connected with the use of the data is that job projections may be overstated, not least during a recession. Furthermore, some of the data is channelled through regional development agencies that may have an interest in inflating figures. At the same time the reported figures on new jobs may also represent an underestimation of employment creation because:

a. The data refers to announced new projects that are known to the IBB. A number of projects (especially expansions) may go ahead without IBB knowledge.
b. The data may be skewed towards manufacturing industry, or to those projects that have actively sought regional financial assistance.

One final problem connected with the use of the IBB data is that the IBB regions classification varies slightly from UK standard regional definitions. As a consequence this analysis will include East Anglia within 'South East'.

In spite of these data problems, Hill and Munday (1992a) conclude that IBB data is the best available at the present time, whilst noting that the paucity of information on the regional distribution of new foreign inward investment is unfortunate given the importance of foreign owned manufacturing and services to the UK.

Table 3.6 Regional new FDI, 1982–92

(a) *New projects*

	1982	1983	1984	1985	1986	1987	1988	1989	1990	1991	1992	Total	Region av.% share
North	5	20	29	26	30	31	22	46	44	31	34	328	10.24
Yorks/Humber	7	10	7	16	11	23	23	11	26	22	42	198	6.10
East Mids	13	12	11	19	15	11	18	11	15	7	5	137	4.56
South East	25	59	70	84	60	55	46	3	7	42	20	491	15.68
South West	7	9	14	15	12	11	5	8	3	6	7	97	3.17
West Mids	1	13	14	63	74	59	69	87	73	50	38	541	15.46
N. West	14	22	40	28	34	28	30	52	53	73	23	397	12.10
Wales	17	31	42	45	49	58	56	42	70	74	61	545	16.60
Scotland	28	49	74	57	36	31	58	34	41	31	61	500	16.09
G. Britain	127	225	301	353	321	307	327	314	332	336	291	3 234	

(b) *New jobs*

	1982	1983	1984	1985	1986	1987	1988	1989	1990	1991	1992	Total	Region av.% share
North	539	1 066	4 589	1 987	1 581	3 491	2 041	4 495	2 714	2 756	2 290	27 549	11.73
Yorks/Humber	104	345	119	2 263	158	1 147	1 790	600	2 464	1 308	1 223	11 521	4.80
East Mids	848	939	658	778	557	456	1 139	4 073	820	766	117	11 151	4.86
South East	1 300	3 036	2 731	3 649	2 118	2 698	2 400	2 163	610	1 794	1 274	23 773	11.27
South West	1 295	451	1 364	1 281	1 129	564	479	1 848	580	790	285	10 066	4.96
West Mids	100	1 201	1 531	5 197	4 393	3 079	3 671	5 629	4 410	2 612	1 508	33 331	13.86
N. West	1 291	709	1 135	2 271	1 400	1 323	1 763	2 646	1 810	1 894	1 105	17 347	8.00
Wales	901	2 166	3 958	2 416	2 364	4 054	6 006	3 664	2 636	6 493	2 357	36 965	16.14
Scotland	2 258	5 135	8 761	4 971	1 881	3 704	5 429	4 551	9 799	3 648	4 497	54 634	24.39
G. Britain	8 636	14 998	24 846	24 813	15 581	20 516	24 718	29 669	25 843	22 061	14 656	226 337	

Source: Invest in Britain Bureau.

Table 3.7   Index of relative regional inward investment performance, 1982–92

(a) New projects

	1982	1983	1984	1985	1986	1987	1988	1989	1990	1991	1992	Index average 1982/92
North	2.27	1.73	1.92	1.44	1.84	1.97	1.34	2.97	2.67	1.86	2.31	2.03
Yorks/Humber	0.64	0.52	0.28	0.53	0.41	0.89	0.84	0.43	0.91	0.76	1.66	0.71
East Mids	1.48	0.77	0.54	0.75	0.66	0.50	0.78	0.50	0.64	0.29	0.24	0.65
South East	0.53	0.69	0.61	0.63	0.49	0.46	0.37	0.19	0.06	0.34	0.19	0.41
South West	0.76	0.54	0.63	0.57	0.49	0.48	0.20	0.33	0.11	0.22	0.30	0.42
West Mids	0.08	0.61	0.50	1.87	2.46	2.00	2.26	3.00	2.34	1.61	1.42	1.65
N. West	0.97	0.87	1.17	0.73	0.96	0.86	0.84	1.51	1.47	1.97	0.72	1.10
Wales	3.07	3.19	3.19	3.05	3.59	4.67	3.93	3.04	4.73	4.86	4.68	3.82
Scotland	2.35	2.36	2.64	1.78	1.25	1.15	2.01	1.23	1.40	1.01	2.25	1.77

(b) *New jobs*

	1982	1983	1984	1985	1986	1987	1988	1989	1990	1991	1992	*Index average 1982/92*
North	1.20	1.38	3.69	1.57	2.00	3.33	1.64	3.07	2.11	2.51	3.10	2.33
Yorks/Humber	0.14	0.27	0.06	1.07	0.12	0.66	0.87	0.25	1.11	0.68	0.96	0.56
East Mids	1.42	0.90	0.39	0.44	0.50	0.31	0.65	1.94	0.45	0.48	0.11	0.69
South East	0.40	0.54	0.29	0.39	0.36	0.34	0.25	0.19	0.06	0.22	0.23	0.30
South West	2.06	0.41	0.74	0.69	0.96	0.37	0.25	0.80	0.28	0.44	0.24	0.66
West Mids	0.12	0.85	0.66	2.20	3.00	1.56	1.59	2.05	1.82	1.28	1.12	1.48
N. West	1.31	0.42	0.40	0.84	0.82	0.61	0.65	0.81	0.64	0.78	0.69	0.72
Wales	2.39	3.27	3.64	2.33	3.57	4.88	5.57	2.80	2.29	6.50	3.59	3.71
Scotland	2.79	3.71	3.78	2.21	1.34	2.05	2.49	1.74	4.29	1.81	3.29	2.68

Note: Index = Annual regional share of FDI new jobs/projects divided by regional share of employment.
Source: Adapted from Invest in Britain Bureau and *Regional Trends*, various.

Table 3.6. shows the number of new projects and associated new jobs going to mainland regions of the UK for each year from 1982 to 1992. Northern Ireland is excluded from this analysis (see Chapter 5). The final column shows the average annual share of projects and new jobs going to these regions over the period 1982–1992. In terms of shares alone, some regions have clearly outperformed others. Between 1982 and 1992 the two Celtic regions, Wales and Scotland, together attracted around 33 per cent of new projects and over 40 per cent of associated new jobs. The West Midlands also appears to have performed well, especially during the later 1980s. Over the whole period the West Midlands attracted around 15 per cent of new jobs and projects coming to the UK. The area was granted Assisted Area status in the mid-1980s, which from this evidence certainly aided the region in its search for foreign capital. The Northern region has also performed well, attracting over 10 per cent of new projects and jobs during the period.

Whilst Table 3.6. says something about likely winning regions, it does not allow a sequential ranking of best performers. For example between 1982 and 1992 the South East region succeeded in attracting 11 per cent of the total number of projects coming to the UK, but the core region is far larger than peripheral regions. Scotland is around a quarter of the size of the South East region in employment terms, yet attracted nearly a sixth of all projects during the period. To compensate for this size effect, and to develop a league table of success, both regional shares of new projects and associated jobs are divided by regional shares of employment to provide a measure of relative regional performance (Table 3.7). An index value of one indicates that the region has attracted a share of incoming foreign projects (and new jobs) commensurate with its employment size. A value higher than 1 indicates the attraction of a share of projects greater than its equivalent employment share.

On the basis of regional performance index averaged for the years 1982–1992 a league table of success is generated (Table 3.8).

On the basis of this league table, four regions clearly stand out, with Wales in particular well ahead of the competition. Analysis

Table 3.8   A league table of inward investment success, 1982–92

Region	Av. 1982–92 project index	Region	Av. 1982–92 new jobs index
Wales	3.82	Wales	3.71
North	2.03	Scotland	2.68
Scotland	1.77	North	2.33
West Midlands	1.65	West Midlands	1.48
North West	1.10	North West	0.72
Yorks/Humber	0.71	East Midlands	0.69
East Midlands	0.65	South West	0.66
South West	0.42	Yorks/Humber	0.56
South East	0.41	South East	0.30

Source: Derived from Invest in Britain data and Regional Trends, various.

will now turn to these winning regions in a little more detail. To date, the concentrations of inward investment in these regions have been addressed from national data. Here it is possible to look more closely at the investment record of these winning regions.

Wales

In terms of the relative regional performance index, Wales has led the race to attract new inward foreign investment. Although Wales is small in respect of its share of UK employment, it has consistently attracted a high share of new foreign projects and jobs. Foreign owned companies have been present in Wales for nearly a century (Hill and Morris, 1991). By the early 1950s, 18 foreign companies in Wales employed around 14 000 people. By 1992, 273 foreign manufacturing companies employed 66 000 people, or around 28 per cent of Welsh manufacturing employment. Recent and accurate data is available in Wales on the extent of foreign firm investment, from the Regional Data System (Welsh Office), and the Welsh Development Agency.

Foreign owned manufacturing in Wales has historically been dominated by North American firms (see Table 3.9). US multinationals in 1992 accounted for just over 32 per cent of the total number of foreign manufacturing units, and 42 per cent of foreign manufacturing employment. This included substantial investments from firms such as Ford (Bridgend), Hoover (Merthyr), Continental Can (Wrexham), Warner Lambert (Pontypool) and Monsanto (Newport and Wrexham). Yet Welsh dependence on North America as a source of international investment has recently reduced considerably. In 1974 North American subsidiary companies in the Welsh economy accounted for 90 per cent of total foreign employment and around 90 per cent of foreign capital invested up to that date.

Table 3.9   Foreign manufacturing plants in Wales, by national origin, 1992

Country	No. of plants	Employment (000s)	(% of foreign total)
USA	112	27.8	(42.1)
Canada	16	4.3	(6.5)
EEC (excl. UK)	110	14.5	(21.9)
of which:			
Germany	41	5.1	(7.7)
France	22	4.5	(6.8)
Other EC	47	4.9	(7.4)
Japan	33	12.2	(18.5)
Sweden	14	1.8	(2.7)
Switzerland	14	1.3	(2.0)
Others	45	4.2	(6.4)
Total	344	66.1	(100.0)

Source: *Welsh Economic Trends*, 1993.

The 1980s, however, saw a significant growth in the number of investments from both the EC and Japan. By 1992 110 EC manufacturing units employed 14 500 people in Wales. These included a significant number of firms in the motor components sector such as Bosch (Miskin) and Valeo (Cefn Hengoed), Alfred Teves (Tredegar), and Gillet Exhausts (Tredegar). By 1992, 33 Japanese manufacturing units in Wales employed just over 12 000 people. Japanese manufacturing investment has grown rapidly since the mid-1980s, as electronics firms have diversified and expanded from initially narrow product bases. Notable among recent investments has been Sony's decision to build a new plant at Pencoed, adding to Sony's significant existing investment at Bridgend, and bringing the firms employment in Wales to around 4000 people.

Table 3.10   Foreign manufacturing in Wales, by broad sector, 1992

Sector	No. of plants	Employment (000's)	% of total
Electrical/electronic and office machinery	60	17.8	(26.9)
Motor vehicle/transport and related components	28	11.0	(16.6)
Chemicals	50	8.3	(12.6)
Metal manufacture and other metal goods	46	7.5	(11.3)
Paper products, printing and publishing	25	4.4	(6.7)
Rubber and plastic	33	3.9	(5.9)
Food and drink	15	2.3	(3.5)
Mechanical engineering	27	2.5	(3.8)
Other sectors	60	8.3	(12.6)
Total	344	66.1	(100.0)

Source: *Welsh Economic Trends*, 1993.

Wales failed to attract the main Toyota car plant, but did succeed in attracting the Toyota engine plant to Deeside in North Wales.

Foreign manufacturing plants and employment classified to industrial sectors are shown in Table 3.10. Over 27 per cent of current foreign manufacturing employment is within the electrical, electronic, office machinery and data processing equipment sectors. Other core sectors include motor vehicles and transport (16 per cent of employment), together with metal manufacture and chemicals. Over time the sectoral distribution of foreign manufacturing employment has followed structural changes in the rest of the Welsh manufacturing sector, that is a reduction in sectoral representation in the more traditional manufacturing elements.

The success of Wales showed no sign of waning even during recession. For example, between 1988 and 1991, a total of 266 new projects by foreign firms were announced with total planned new and safeguarded jobs of nearly 33 000, and planned capital investment of just over £2.6bn (Table 3.11). This latter figure includes the massive Ford engine plant investment at Bridgend. Deducting this figure of over £700m would bring the contribution of European and Japanese investors to the local economy into sharper focus.

In the early 1990s Wales remains the number one performing region, attracting around 20 per cent of total new foreign projects entering the UK annually. Recent success has included the

Table 3.11   Recent Welsh success, 1988–91

Source	New projects	Planned jobs	Planned investment (£m)
N.America	109	15 397	1 456.010
Japan/Asia	47	5 884	476.974
Europe	110	11 595	679.739
Total	266	32 876	2 612.723

Note: During 1992 Wales attracted a further 61 foreign projects with associated new and safeguarded employment of around 6700.

Source: Welsh Development International.

£147m Sony investment at Pencoed creating 1400 jobs and making the site the Sony European TV headquarters, and Dow Corning's £150m factory at Barry Dock. The causes of Welsh success, according to Dr Gwyn Jones of the WDA, are:

a. The business success of existing overseas investors in Wales,
b. The presence of blue chip foreign companies including Sony, Toyota and Bosch,
c. The productivity of the Welsh workforce (noted as being particularly important to Japanese firms),
d. Effective teamwork, the identification of what investors need, and the close cooperation of the WDA, Welsh Office, local authorities and TECs in creating a package for the investor. (Welsh Development Agency, press release, 15.7.92).

The importance of these factors had been noted by other surveys (Arthur D. Little, 1986; Munday, 1990). Wales has been very effectively marketed abroad by the Welsh Development Agency's inward investment arm, Welsh Development International, which has offices in North America, Asia and the EC. However, the success of Wales can also be attributed to definite locational characteristics. Wales is one of the closest UK Assisted Areas to the South East and the Channel Tunnel. Wales offers easy market access for firms looking to the large consumer markets of the South East of England, and to the core areas of the EC. New investors in the Assisted Areas are able to apply for Regional Selective Assistance and a number of other financial incentives. Furthermore, manufacturing earnings in Wales are amongst the lowest in the UK (Simpson, 1992), and there is evidence that the availability of semi-skilled female labour coupled with low female activity rates in Wales has also been a factor in Welsh success (Hill and Munday, 1991; Dunning 1986).

Scotland

Competition between Wales and Scotland to play host to foreign investors has been intense for much of the 1980s. To date however, Scotland has failed to catch Wales in the 'inward investment game', although it has been argued by Young (1989) that the smaller quantity of new inward investment entering Scotland has been superior in quality. Wales and Scotland bear many similarities in terms of the economic and institutional environment. Both regions have well established development agencies with specialist arms to deal with incoming investment. The Scottish equivalent of Welsh Development International is Locate in Scotland, which was formed in 1981 to be a 'one door' inward investment operation charged with marketing Scotland to the outside world. In April 1991 Locate in Scotland (LIS) became a joint operation of both Scottish Enterprise and the Scottish Office. As is the case with its Welsh counterpart, LIS has a network of offices abroad, advises inward investors, negotiates development packages as well as providing post investment services. Effective marketing, tailored financial incentives, labour and premises availability have to some extent made up for the disadvantages Scotland faces in being distant from large consumer markets, with no high speed link to the North of England.

Between 1982 and 1992 Scotland attracted a total of 500 new foreign projects with associated planned new employment of over 24 000 (Table 3.6). However, LIS itself believes that these planned employment figures require discounting by something like two-thirds in reaching actual new employment out-turns (LIS, 1991). Between 1981 and 1991 the planned investment by new inward investors (including UK) in Scotland totalled around £4.65bn.

North America is the key source of both new and existing foreign investment in Scotland, reflected by the fact that Locate in Scotland maintains four offices in the US. Between 1988 and 1991, North American investment accounted for over 50 per cent of new foreign projects and planned jobs, and just over 70 per cent of planned foreign investment (Table 3.12). This reflects recent investment by US firms such as Health Care International (Hospital development, Clydebank), Tandy Corporation (Consumer electronics, East Kilbride), and Motorola (Research and Development Centre, Livingstone).

Table 3.12   New inward investment in Scotland, 1988–91

Source	Projects	Planned jobs	Planned investment (£m)
N. America	73	13 399	1 037
Japan/Asia	24	4 157	257
Europe (excl. UK)	45	5 554	180
UK	99	14 361	590
Total foreign	142	23 110	1 474
Grand total	241	37 471	2 064

Sector	Planned investment (£m)
Electronics	1 124
Engineering	360
Chemical, plastics, rubber	148
Textiles	64
Services	62
Others	306*
Total	2 064

Note: *nearly 60 per cent of this figure is made up by one investment: the Health Care International 1991 investment in a hospital at Clydebank.

Source: Locate in Scotland, *Annual Reports*, 1991–2.

The largest foreign concentration in terms of industrial sector is in electronics and engineering. The foreign electronics industry has been the main target for Scotland's promotional agencies. During the late 1970s the Scottish Development Agency hoped that the region would become Europe's equivalent of Silicon Valley in the US. By then Scotland already had an existing mass of US electronics firms. By attracting new MNE electronics firms, Scotland could acquire a critical mass alowing a fully integrated industry segment to develop. Although a large number of electronics firms did enter the Scottish economy during the 1980s, the adjudged critical mass has not yet occurred, although some have argued that Scotland still has the ingredients for hi-tec success (Maremont, 1989). During the early 1990s, Silicon Glen has been exposed to demand shifts in the world computer industry. Unisys, for example, has closed its Livingstone plant with 700 job losses, and although Silicon Glen has so far been spared serious closures, there is a fear that inward investment in hi-tec sectors is vulnerable (Buxton, 1992). Ian Lang, Scottish Secretary said:

'We should never assume that inward investment is the answer to all our prayers. It is a high risk strategy in the sense that high-tech industry has a shorter shelf life. It is susceptible to recession, and more so to obsolescense, and the combination (of the two) can be very serious indeed' (Lang, in Buxton,1992).

Other commentators have been more scathing. There has been some debate in Scotland as to the extent to which foreign electronics firms are creating a low grade off-shore assembly platform for MNEs anxious to break into the EC market (Evans, 1989). The extent to which foreign firms can contribute to regional development is dealt with further in the next chapter.

West Midlands

As with other 'winning regions' the West Midlands economy was originally based around a few core industries which declined rapidly in the late 1970s, leaving a trail of industrial dereliction and unemployment, notably through the Black Country and its environs. The West Midlands as a region however, takes in more than just the metropolitan county, and includes the counties of Staffordshire, Shropshire, Hereford and Worcester, as well as Warwickshire. Multinational enterprise has been present in the West Midlands for many years and it has been argued that multinational enterprise investment strategies during the 1970s, especially the drive to find least cost production locations overseas, contributed significantly to the problems the region faced during the early 1980s (Gaffikon and Nickson, 1984).

In spite of changes in the foreign owned segments of West Midlands industry, foreign manufacturers maintained overall employment during the 1980s at around 70 000 people (Business Monitor, PA1002), or 10 per cent of West Midlands manufacturing employment. However, between 1989 and 1990 foreign manufacturing employment in West Midlands grew by around 20 000, and foreign manufacturing employment now represents nearly 14 per cent of the regions manufacturing employment.

Between 1982 and 1992 the West Midlands attracted over 540 foreign projects, with associated new employment of just over 33 000 people (Table 3.6). Since 1984 foreign direct investment in the region has exceeded £2.5bn (WMDA, 1992). In terms of the performance index, it can be seen that the region attracted a higher proportion of UK foreign projects and jobs from 1985 onwards. During 1984 the core area of the West Midlands succeeded in attaining intermediate area status. Also during 1984, the West Midlands Industrial Development Association (WMIDA, now WMDA) was formed to coordinate the marketing of the region to foreign companies.

It seems likely that because of some combination of these factors, a higher proportion of projects entering the West Midlands became known to the IBB than had previously been the case. For example, this might have occurred as such inward investors applied for financial assistance. Collis and Roberts (1992) showed that a number of foreign investors established prior to 1984 felt that the availability of financial assistance influenced their level of further investment in the region.

The addition of intermediate status has certainly complemented a number of attractive locational characteristics. The West Midlands is centrally located, with reasonable communications to the South East and the EC. The majority of industrial sites are within five hours of the new Channel Tunnel. Good transport and rail communications are supplemented by the cost and availability of industrial floorspace, and by the skills of the local workforce. Collis *et al.* (1989), in a survey of new foreign locators in the West Midlands, found that all the above factors were cited by the companies as being important in final site decisions. Interestingly, in this survey the availability of financial assistance was ranked low by new locators. The cost of labour in the West Midlands is low in comparison to other areas of the UK, with the average gross weekly earnings of full time men being only 90 per cent of the Great Britain average (*Regional Trends*, 1992).

Around half of foreign investment is located within the Metropolitan area, with the remainder spread evenly among the four non-metropolitan counties (Collis *et al.*, 1988). However, the sectoral composition of this FOC investment varies across the region. Collis *et al.* (1988) found that warehousing and distribution together with sales and marketing, accounted for around two-thirds of the number of foreign firms in 1987, with 130 firms engaged in manufacture, assembly and research/development. The Collis *et al.* (1989) survey of new foreign locators in the West Midlands confirmed the prominence of projects in distribution (54 per cent) and in metals engineering and vehicles (34 per cent).

Collis and Roberts (1992), referring to their survey work on inward investment in the West Midlands, found that most FOCs carry out a wide variety of functions (Table 3.13), and that there was some tendency for FOCs to initially conduct sales and marketing activities before turning to manufacture.

In terms of countries of origin, Collis and Roberts showed that between 1984 and 1986, 42 per cent of new projects were of

Table 3.13   Types of activity of West Midlands FOCs

Activity	Total % 1987	Total % 1989
Component manufacture	23	24
Final product manufacture	36	17
Final product assembly	28	26
Research and development	32	20
Warehousing	32	31
Warehousing and distribution	48	49
Servicing	48	37
Sales and marketing	87	74

Source: Collis and Roberts, 1992.

North American origin, with 34 per cent from the EC and 12 per cent from the Far East. It was concluded that the West Midlands had a higher proportion of EC investment than other UK standard regions. In 1989 39 per cent of the West Midlands stock of FOCs originated from the EC, compared to 37 per cent of North American origin. Reducing dependence on North America as a source of foreign inward investment has also been noted by Hill and Munday (1992b) in relation to the Welsh economy.

Among EC investors in the West Midlands it is Germany that has been the most important. In 1991 there were 145 German-owned companies spread through the region, including firms such as Lindemann Machine, Grundig International, INA Bearing, TRW Valves and Thyssen (Feddersen, 1991). Wells (1992) specifically considers the importance of German investment in the West Midlands automotive sector and its implications for local development.

Japanese investment has also become increasingly important to the West Midlands. By 1991/92, there were 60 Japanese firms established in the region employing over 8300 people (WMDA, 1992). The Telford area in particular has attracted a high levels of Japanese investment, and by 1990 could boast the presence of such names as Epson (personal computers/printers), Maxell, NEC (fax machines, printers and monitors) and Ricoh (copiers and fax machines). By 1990 Japanese investment in Telford had passed the £100m level, and these four firms alone employed 2300 people (EIAJ, 1990). A further boost for the West Midlands was the decision by Yamazaki to build a showcase factory at Worcester, making machining centres.

There is every sign that the West Midlands will continue to be an important location for inward investors. A survey completed by KPMG Peat Marwick in association with the West Midlands Development Agency in 1992 looked at 344 (of the 700) foreign companies in the West Midlands, employing between them 68 000 people, and showed that these companies alone had capital expenditure plans for the year totalling £147m, with over two thirds of this investment coming from the US, Germany and Japan.

Collis and Roberts concluded by examining the impact of FOCs on the West Midlands economy, to show that the contributions have been;

a. The development of a skills base, aided through the training activities of FOCs,
b. Local purchases of capital equipment,
c. The use of local services,
d. Helping to restructure the local economy away from the problems of the early 1980s.

In the West Midlands at least, there is strong evidence of a substantial local economic impact attributable to the presence of foreign investment.

Northern Region

Northern region takes in not only the old industrial areas of Teesside and Tyne and Wear, but also Northumberland, Durham and Cumbria. The economy of the North East in particular was traditionally concentrated in a few narrow industrial segments, most notably, shipbuilding, coal and steel. Shipbuilding has now virtually disappeared, and severe structural changes through the seventies and 1980s have left Northern region with the highest mainland unemployment rates. Between 1976 and 1986 the number of employees in employment in Northern fell by 194 000 (15 per cent). Inward foreign investment has been crucial in attempts to reduce these high levels of unemployment, and the severe social problems of the area that were highlighted during the riots on Tyneside during September 1991.

In 1990 foreign manufacturing industry employed nearly 50 000 people in Northern, which represented 4.4 per cent of total regional employment and 17 per cent of manufacturing employment. Throughout the 1980s foreign manufacturing has become more important to the region. It is one of the only regions where foreign manufacturing has grown as a proportion of total employ-

ment through the 1980s. In terms of the relative regional performance index Northern has attracted a consistently high proportion of
new foreign projects. National press and academic comment on
inward investment in Northern has been concentrated largely
around Japanese investors. The jewel in the crown for Northern
was the decision of Nissan to locate in Sunderland during 1984.
This was an investment of substantial economic significance,
being the largest Japanese inward investment to enter the EC to
that date. Investment at the Nissan plant by 1992 has reached
around £900m. The projected employment for 1993 is 4600 people
with a production level of 300 000 cars. The 'Nissan effect' has
however gone beyond direct employment creation alone. Nissan
has succeeded in putting Tyne and Wear on the European inward
investment map, and has contributed to the general pull of the area.
A number of investors have come to the North East specifically to
serve the Nissan plant including Ikeda Hoover, TI-Nihon, SP Tyres
and Nissan Yamoto. Whilst press and academic comment has
centred on Nissan there are a number of other Japanese firms in the
region including significant investments by Komatsu (Birtley),
NSK (Peterlee) and Fujitsu (Newton Aycliffe). The Fujitsu investment announced during 1989 will create over 1500 jobs in a
£400m plant producing semiconductors. The Northern Development Corporation believes that by 1993 Japanese investment in
Northern region will have created 12 000 jobs and led to investment of over £1.4bn (Northern Development Corporation, 1992).

As has been the case in Wales and the West Midlands, Japanese
and European investments are becoming more and more important. Major European investments include BASF (chemicals),
NEI/ABB (power stations), Valeo (automotive components) and
Nestlé. There are also a number of Scandinavian investments,
most notably, Electrolux (Sweden), Grundfos (Denmark) and
Norsk Hydro (Norway). Electrolux alone employs over 2000
people in the region making cookers, refridgerators, and mowers.

In the 18 months to 1991 inward investors started 83 projects
with around £1bn of capital spending, and 8000 new or safeguarded jobs. Of these, 37 were European, 24 were from the Far

East (and accounted for 40 per cent of the planned jobs), with only 22 from the US.

Despite excitement over growing Japanese investment levels, there are fears that the performance of the North during the 1990s will not replicate her performance in the 1980s. The Northern Development Corporation expects the weakening of the yen, the Single European market, and stronger regional competition for inward investment to affect Northern region performance. As projects become more capital intensive, it is believed that investors will seek highly skilled labour, which core areas of the EC may be able to provide. The Northern region may then be faced with a need to target new Japanese sectors and to tap new Far Eastern sources for inward investment (Northern Development Corporation Economic Research Office, 1992).

The next chapter will now consider more generally the characteristics of regions that have influenced relative inward investment, and will go on to examine the influence of inward investment on regional economic development.

References

Arthur, D. Little Limited (1986), *A Survey of Foreign Firms in Wales*, Cardiff: Wales Investment Location.

Buxton, J. (1992), 'Lang warns Scottish electronics industry', *Financial Times*, 19.5.92, p. 7.

Collis, C. and Roberts, P. (1992), 'FDI in the West Midlands: An Analysis and Evaluation', *Local Economy*, 7.2, 114–30.

Collis, C., Noon, D., Berkeley, N. and Roberts, P. (1989), *Overseas Investment in the West Midlands Region* (second report), report commissioned by the West Midlands Industrial Development Association.

Collis, C., Roberts, P., Noon, D. and Irving, P. (1988), *Overseas Investment in the West Midlands Region*, Coventry Polytechnic, Department of Urban and Regional Planning.

Dunning, J. H. (1986), *Japanese Participation in British Industry*, London: Croom Helm.

Electronics Industry Association of Japan (EIAJ) (1990), *Investment in Britain by Japan's Electronics Industry*, London: EIAJ.

Evans, R. (1989), 'Silicon Quandary', International Management UK, 44.10, 68–9.

Feddersen, K. (1991), *German Subsidiary Companies in the UK*, London: German Chamber of Industry and Commerce.

Gaffikon, F. and Nickson, A. (1984), *Job Crisis in the Multinationals: The Case of the West Midlands*, Birmingham: Birmingham Trade Union Group for World Development and Birmingham Trade Union Resource Centre.

Hill, S. and Morris, J. (1991), *Wales in the 1990s*, London: EIU.

Hill, S. and Munday, M. (1991), 'Why are Welsh Wages so Low?', *Welsh Economic Review*, 4.1, 53–9.

Hill, S. and Munday, M. (1992a), 'The Regional Distribution of Foreign Direct Investment in the UK', *Regional Studies*, 26.6, 535–44.

Hill, S. and Munday, M. (1992b), 'Japanese Investment: The Benefits for Wales', *Anglo-Japanese Economic Journal*, 6.1. 12, 15.

Income Data Services (1990), *Report 619*.

KPMG Peat Marwick (1992), *Survey of Foreign Owned Firms in the West Midlands*, Birmingham: West Midlands Development Association.

Locate In Scotland (1991), *Review 1990–91*, Glasgow: Scottish Enterprise.

Locate in Scotland (1992), *Review 1991 and 1992*, Glasgow: Scottish Enterprise.

Maremont, M. (1989)', Scotland's Silicon Glen? Not Yet', *Business Week*, 3132, p. 152.

McDermott, P. J. (1977), 'Overseas Investment and the Industrial Geography of the UK', *Area*, 9, 200–207.

Munday, M. (1990), *Japanese Manufacturing Investment in Wales*, Cardiff: University of Wales Press.

Northern Development Corporation (1992), *International Investment in the North of England*, Newcastle: Northern Development Corporation.

Northern Development Corporation Economic Research Office (1992), *Business Review North*, vol. 4, Newcastle: Northern Development Corporation.

Simpson, D. (1992), 'Why are Welsh wages so Low? II', *Welsh Economic Review*, 5.1, 54–63.

Watts, H. D. (1982), 'The Inter-Regional Distribution of West German Multinationals in the UK', in M. Taylor and N. Thrift (eds) *The Geography of Multinationals*, London: Croom Helm.

Wells, P. (1992), 'European FDI and Local Development: The Case of the Automotive Sector', *Local Economy*, 7.2, 132–45.

West Midlands Development Agency (1992), *Annual Report*, Birmingham: WMDA.

Young, S. (1989), 'Scotland v. Wales in the Inward Investment Game', *Fraser of Allander Institute Quarterly Economic Commentary*, 14.3, 59–63.

4 Regional Economic Development and Inward Investment

4.1 INTRODUCTION

Earlier chapters have demonstrated the uneven nature of the regional distribution of recent FDI in Britain. The purpose of this chapter is to place that distribution within the context of the economic needs of regions, and to examine more closely the relationship between FDI and regional economic development. All British regions have sought, with varying degrees of success, to attract foreign manufacturing investment, and there is widespread recognition, particularly in a UK context, of the potential of FDI to reduce regional disparities and promote regional economic development (see, for example, Morris, 1987).

This chapter will examine the various means by which national and local authorities have attempted to influence the location of inward investment, with some consideration of the efficacy of these efforts. Later empirical evidence will show that Regional Preferential Assistance (that is, government expenditure on assistance to industry in Assisted Areas), has been an important influence on the distribution of recent inward investment, although tempered by the pervasive influence of other regional economic characteristics.

The first step in any consideration of the regional impact of inward investment must be some analysis, however brief, of the economic needs of regions, in order to provide a framework for assessment. This will be followed by a short review of regional policy in Britain and the EC, and how such policy attempts to influence the location of industries and hence employment. The economic case for and against government intervention in the regional allocation of economic activity will be considered, as well as the nature of those regional economic characteristics that may be expected to influence industrial location. The chapter will conclude by examining the role of inward investment in both regional policy and regional economic development.

4.2   THE ECONOMIC NEEDS OF REGIONS

The Local Government Act of 1972 was the most recent revision of the UK regional definitions, delineating eleven Standard Planning Regions, used as the area basis for official data collection and publication. The Standard Planning Regions can currently be further sub-divided into 46 counties (including seven Metropolitan Areas), although the Boundary Commission is currently reviewing Local Authority areas with a view to introducing Unitary Authorities (that is, combining the responsibilities of counties and districts). Whilst part of the justification for regional definition is economic, interregional linkages in the movement of goods and people means that the definition of regions in Britain relies more heavily on historical, cultural and political issues than on economic ones. Nevertheless each region has its own economic identity in terms of characteristics such as prosperity, industrial structure, employment, etc., and it is differences in economic characteristics which define the 'regional problem' in Britain in the sense of regional economic disparities which are seen as either unfair or inefficient or both.

This 'regional problem' may have many dimensions, but is customarily characterised in terms of levels of unemployment, incomes and spending, and in terms of dependence on a narrow industrial base, low levels of infrastructure or skills and high levels of outward migration. Notice that it is generally deviations away from a national average, rather than absolute levels of some summary economic variable that defines the 'regional problem'.

Figure 4.1 presents a map of the 11 Standard Planning Regions of the UK, whilst Table 4.1 sets out some economic indicators of

Source: *Regional Trends*.

Figure 4.1   Map of Standard Planning Regions

Table 4.1   Regional economic disparities, 1981 and 1991 (UK = 100)

| | GDP/head | | Unemployment rate | | Manufacturing as % of regional GDP | |
	1981	1991	1981	1991	1981	1991
North	93.5	89.1	130	129	121.8	131.4
Yorks/Humber	92.0	91.6	104	107	113.9	118.6
East Midlands	96.9	98.1	90	89	125.1	128.1
East Anglia	96.4	100.4	81	72	102.8	101.4
South East	117.1	116.5	71	86	88.9	72.9
South West	93.3	94.2	87	88	95.4	89.1
West Midlands	90.6	92.0	120	106	143.1	140.0
North West	94.3	92.7	122	117	126.9	130.0
Wales	83.6	86.5	128	107	91.1	121.4
Scotland	96.3	96.7	120	107	102.1	94.8
N Ireland	78.8	77.1	159	169	83.9	83.3
UK	£3 653	£8 516	9.5%	8.0%	24.8%	21.0%

Sources: *Regional Trends, Economic Trends*, various.

the 'regional problem'. Comparison of 1981 with 1991 shows the persistence of regional differences. For example, the range of relative regional GDP per head in 1991 (highest minus lowest) was virtually identical to that in 1981, whilst the range of relative unemployment rates had actually increased over the period. The final columns show the relative importance of manufacturing as a share of GDP in each region, demonstrating the role of the Midlands and North as the manufacturing heartlands of Britain.

Whilst Table 4.1 gives some indication of regional differences in aggregate terms, Table 4.2 shows how these translate into indicators of personal economic well-being, demonstrating if anything even wider disparities. Although a gently progressive income tax structure and a system of social security benefits mean that disposable income disparities are narrower than earnings differences, the correlation between low relative participation rates, together with the concentration of wealth into high earning regions, serve to open up personal income differences between regions. By 1991

Table 4.2   Regional economic disparities: incomes and earnings, 1981 and 1991

	GB = 100 Average gross weekly earnings		UK = 100 Regional disposable income/head		UK = 100 Social security as share of household income	
	April 1981	April 1991	1981	1991	1981	1991
North	96.5	90.6	94.8	91.3	128.6	146.3
Yorks/Humber	95.5	90.6	93.5	93.1	126.2	125.9
East Midlands	94.9	91.8	96.6	95.8	93.7	97.2
East Anglia	96.6	94.5	97.0	98.0	98.4	91.2
South East	108.0	114.8	114.4	113.7	75.4	70.4
South West	95.0	93.3	97.4	94.6	112.7	88.9
West Midlands	94.3	91.7	88.3	91.8	95.2	114.8
North West	96.8	93.8	94.9	95.3	108.7	117.6
Wales	95.6	88.6	89.5	85.7	131.8	149.1
Scotland	97.7	93.2	95.9	100.5	110.3	125.9
N Ireland	–	–	84.4	86.4	174.6	152.8
UK (GB)	£124.9	£284.7	£3 125	£7 071	12.6%	10.8%

Sources: *Regional Trends, Welsh Economic Trends*, various.

average personal disposable incomes in the highest average income region were 30 per cent higher than in the lowest income region. The North, Wales and Northern Ireland each had average disposable incomes that were more than 10 per cent below the UK average. Tables 4.1 and 4.2, taken together, show that relatively low average incomes go hand in hand with low levels of GDP per head, and high levels of unemployment with greater dependency on social security as a source of household income.

On the basis of data such as Table 4.1 and 4.2, it is possible to group regions into a core, an inner periphery and an outer periphery (see, for example, Griffiths and Wall, 1989, and Northern Ireland Economic Research Centre, 1992).

The core area, with the highest levels of prosperity, consists of the South East, East Midlands and East Anglia. The inner periphery comprises of the West Midlands, South West and Yorks/

Humberside, leaving the North West, North, Wales, Scotland and Northern Ireland as outer peripheral regions in both geographical and economic senses. However, it must be noted that inter-regional flows of economic activity, including the movement of both goods and factors, are reducing the validity of regional groupings, with national and multinational enterprises increasingly seen as 'footloose' and able to choose locations on the basis of local economic characteristics in order to maximise advantage or minimise cost. Rapid improvements in technology and infra-structure have reduced the need to locate in the proximity of major product (and even factor) markets, allowing companies to locate on peripheral greenfield sites, unencumbered by traditional practices in production and employment. These technical and logistical improvements increasingly permit location away from the manufacturing heartland without significant transport cost penalties. In theory this 'footloose' nature of new manufacturing investment will ultimately reduce regional economic differences; in practice data such as Tables 4.1 and 4.2 provide little evidence of such effects to date.

4.3   ECONOMIC POLICY AND REGIONAL DEVELOPMENT

There are inevitably a wide variety of theories which seek to explain the existence and persistence of regional economic differences, with some dispute over whether market forces will narrow or exacerbate these differences (see for example, Hill and Minford, 1993). The existence of regional differences is perhaps easier to explain than their persistence. Given that each region has its own unique industrial employment structure, changes in the pattern of demand will have a differing impact on regions. For example, the international decline in the demand for steel in recent years has had disproportionate impact on the steel-producing regions (the North East, Scotland, and Wales), whilst the end of the 'Cold War' and subsequent decline in defence spending has had its disproportionate impact on the defence-intensive regions of the South East and South West.

Proponents of the free market have argued that, given time, the market will eliminate regional disparities as firms move into low wage/high unemployment regions in order to reduce labour costs, whilst labour in these regions moves to high wage/low unemployment areas. In other words, other things being equal, mobile capital and labour will move to take advantage of any regional differences in factor rewards. As firms move into low wage/high unemployment regions, wages and employment will both increase. Ultimately, market forces will lead factors to relocate in order to equalise factor rewards, thereby causing regional economic convergence (see, for example, Hardwick, Khan and Langmead, 1990).

In practice, markets are necessarily imperfect, with restrictions on the mobility of labour, capital and other inputs, whilst other things are not necessarily equal across regions. Market imperfections can include a lack of knowledge about opportunities as well as transaction costs in the physical movement of workers and their families, or in the movement of capital. Added to these private transaction cost constraints on factor mobility are the social and public costs of the resource misallocation that occurs when local economies change quickly. In addition, market forces may even act to widen regional divides. For example, whilst factor rewards may encourage labour to move from low wage/high unemployment regions, the sort of labour that is most likely to move is young and skilled, leaving behind an ageing and less productive workforce that is hardly attractive to firms contemplating relocation. As regional output and incomes decline so does the ability of the community to finance the infrastructure necessary to attract new firms, whilst an ageing and increasingly dependent population imposes mounting pressure on local services. From this perspective, central and local governments need to act, both to enhance factor mobility and to influence its pattern of use, by encouraging new and relocating firms into less prosperous regions. In this way economic divergence is reduced, hence breaking the cycle of regional disparities in which relatively poor regions lose their most productive people and fail to generate sufficient local demand and incomes to encourage firms to stay or move in, and are caught in a downward spiral of declining incomes, services, infrastructure and population.

Britain has long recognised the need for intervention in the 'regional problem', beginning with the Special Areas Act of 1934, but the enthusiasm of successive governments for regional policy has waxed and waned over the years since. The essence of Britain's regional policy has been to identify areas needing assistance and then to develop schemes to encourage firms to move into the designated areas, to encourage existing firms in these areas to grow and to discourage the growth of firms outside of the designated areas. The level and range of assistance and control has varied substantially. Not surprisingly, Labour governments have been rather more enthusiastic about regional policy and have been ready to combine financial aid with physical controls on development, whilst Conservative governments have been more content to 'encourage' markets to work more effectively, with generally lower levels of financial help to firms moving into designated areas.

4.4   GOVERNMENT AID TO REGIONS

Parts of Britain eligible for aid (preferential assistance) under regional policy are denoted as Assisted Areas, currently covering around 35 per cent of the British workforce. Assisted Areas are divided into two categories; Development Areas (eligible for most aid), with about 15 per cent of the British workforce, and Intermediate Areas with 20 per cent of the workforce. The current map of Assisted Areas is shown in Figure 4.2, revised in July 1993. The previous review took place in 1984, resulting in parts of the West Midlands joining the Assisted Areas. The July 1993 review added parts of the South East to the Assisted Areas map. Designation is left to Ministerial discretion, although having

Figure 4.2   Map of Assisted Areas

'regard to all circumstances actual and expected including the state of employment and unemployment, population changes, migration and the objectives of regional policy' (Review of Assisted Areas, Department of Trade and Industry Briefing, 1992).

The major shifts in Regional Policy in the past decade have been reductions in the overall level of assistance, and away from automatic, mandatory assistance for eligible projects and towards discretionary aid. In 1988 the UK government ended automatic regional grants. The primary remaining form of aid to Assisted Areas is Regional Selective Assistance (RSA) introduced in the Industry Act, 1972, subsequently amended by the Industrial Development Act of 1982. RSA is a discretionary project related capital grant (although it may include exchange risk cover and low interest loans from the European Coal and Steel Community Loan Fund), which may be available to new qualifying projects in the Assisted Areas. The size of any RSA grant is limited to the minimum of three ceilings:

- a maximum internal Net Grant Equivalent (NGE), believed to be currently 30 per cent of eligible project costs in Development Areas, and 20 per cent in Intermediate Areas;
- a maximum cost per job, believed to be 5500 European Currency Units (ECUs), per job in Development Areas and 3500 ECUs in Intermediate Areas.
- European Commission limits on maximum assistance under competition rules.

Eligible projects in Assisted Areas must meet certain conditions. Projects must be viable (that is will require assistance once only), must create or safeguard employment, should lead to a substantial improvement in performance and should strengthen the regional and national economies. Projects must meet an additionality condition, that is the project must demonstrate the need for assistance (would not go ahead without it), with the grant being limited to the minimum necessary to allow the project to proceed. In practice this means that the level of grant is subject to negotiation, while projects that simply displace employment elsewhere (either regionally or nationally) are unlikely to qualify for grant aid.

Whilst the level of RSA award to individual projects is not normally disclosed, in the financial year 1989/90, 1545 RSA offers were made promising assistance totalling £265m, whilst actual payments made summed to £175m, given to projects involving 57 000 jobs, of which three-quarters were categorised as new, one-quarter as safeguarded. In any year RSA offers are likely to exceed actual payments, since some offers may be declined, whilst actual payment is staggered to follow project development. In the year 1988/89, the average RSA grant offer was 11.3 per cent of total eligible project costs, although this percentage was relatively high compared to previous years. All figures in this paragraph are from the *Journal of Regional Policy*, 12, 3–4, December 1992.

In April 1988 the British Government introduced the Regional Enterprise Grant, available in one of two forms to small firms (less than 25 employees) in the Development Areas. The Investment Grant provides up to 15 per cent of eligible capital expenditure for small projects, with a maximum grant of £15 000. The Innovation Grant provides up to 50 per cent of eligible expenditure for products involving new innovation in terms of product or processes, up to a maximum grant of £25 000.

Finally, the special circumstances of Northern Ireland have led to the entire region being given Special Development Area status, with a wide variety of assistance being available. Consequently, Northern Ireland, with less than 3 per cent of the population, received an average of 14 per cent of total UK spending on Regional Aid in the three years to 1990.

The distribution of government spending on Regional Aid schemes is shown in Table 4.3. RDG refers to Regional Development Grant, a mandatory scheme providing automatic assistance in the form of a capital grant for (typically 15 per cent of the value of) capital equipment (including plant and buildings) in

Table 4.3 Regional aid in Britain: committed expenditure, 1985–9 (£m)

		1985	1986	1987	1988	1989
Britain	RDG	358.4	513.5	270.6	297.4	203.9
	RSA	212.0	183.1	242.6	247.9	265.1
	REG	–	–	–	11.0	18.3
Total GB		570.4	696.6	513.2	556.3	487.3
Northern Ireland		122.4	98.3	89.0	90.8	77.6
Total UK		692.8	794.9	602.2	647.1	564.9

Source: *Journal of Regional Policy*, 12, 3–4, Dec. 92, p. 113.

Development Areas. Whilst RDG was being phased out in the late 1980s, the table shows the impact of staged payments that were agreed several years earlier.

Over the period 1985–9, government spending on regional aid declined substantially, with the steady rise in RSA failing to off-set the erosion of RDG. Figures in Table 4.3 refer to current terms, so that inflation over the period will have accelerated the real reduction in aid. This reduction is consistent with the govern-ment's determination to both bring public expenditure under con-trol (that is reduce it), and to provide an environment in which markets are able to operate more freely.

Not surprisingly, this reduction in government expenditure on regional aid had had a differential impact on regions. Table 4.4 sets out the regional distribution of expenditure on Regional Pref-erential Assistance to industry for the period 1984/5 to 1991/2. Notice that Table 4.4 refers to financial years whilst Table 4.3 shows expenditure in calendar years – hence the tables are only loosely comparable.

Table 4.4 shows the familiar pattern of decline in government expenditure on regional aid since 1986. However the table also shows the changing regional distribution of this aid. In 1984/5, Wales and Scotland accounted for just over a half of all RPA

Table 4.4   Government expenditure on regional preferential assistance to industry, 1984–91 (£m)

	1984/5	85/6	86/7	87/8	88/9	89/90	90/91	91/92
North	125.5	96.6	137.3	109.3	134.1	117.0	85.0	63.8
Yorks/Humber	44.3	36.4	41.9	38.8	50.2	32.4	29.4	18.2
East Midlands	11.4	8.8	10.7	9.4	8.8	9.5	5.5	2.6
East Anglia	0.0	0.0	0.0	0.0	0.0	0.0	0.0	0.0
South East	0.0	0.0	0.0	0.0	0.0	0.0	0.0	0.0
South West	14.6	12.3	23.0	14.8	14.7	10.7	9.0	8.3
West Midlands*	0.0	7.1	10.6	19.3	26.2	19.9	18.0	8.7
North West	106.4	87.5	129.6	79.0	82.3	74.3	57.5	49.5
Wales	147.5	138.4	150.7	132.4	148.2	131.7	133.7	153.9
Scotland	187.1	197.0	242.4	153.2	151.2	144.6	159.1	128.9
GB	636.8	584.1	746.2	556.2	615.7	540.1	497.2	433.9

Note   *Parts of West Midlands were granted Assisted Area status in November 1984.

Sources: *Regional Trends*, 28, Table 13.7, p. 144, 1993.

expenditure; by 1991/2 this share had increased to almost two-thirds. Meanwhile the North plus North West have steadily lost shares of British regional aid, from well over a third in 1984/5 to just over a quarter in 1991/2. By this latter year less than 10 per cent of British regional assistance was being spent outside these four regions, despite the growth in spending on the West Midlands following the acquisition of Assisted Area status to some parts in 1984.

4.5   REGIONAL POLICY AND THE EUROPEAN COMMUNITY

Whilst regional aid schemes vary considerably across Europe, the European Community has taken steps towards both harmonisation and the promotion of economic development in poorer regions within the EC context. Table 4.5 provides a summary of regional aid coverage and expenditure across community countries in 1989. Coverage refers to the proportion of the national workforce employed in areas eligible for regional assistance, whilst expenditure is expressed in £s per head of national population, expressed in terms of 1989 Purchasing Power Parity. Of thirteen EC countries only the Netherlands and Denmark have less than a third of the national working population employed in areas eligible for regional aid, whilst for Luxembourg and Portugal the entire country was eligible for regional aid. Regional Aid expenditure per capita varied from less than £1 per head in Denmark to £57 per head in Italy. Not

Table 4.5   Regional aid (1991) and GDP/head (1990) in the EC 12

| Country | Regional Aid | | 1990 GDP/head EC12 average = 100 | | |
	Start 1991 Coverage[1]	Per capita Spending 1989 £s[2]	National	Poorest region	
Belgium	33	12.7	105.0	84.6	(Region Wallone)
Denmark	>0	0.8	107.3	–	
France	<39	1.7	111.5	91.4	(Nord Pas de Calais)
Germany	40	10.2	117.0[3]	98.5[4]	(Schleswig-Holstein)
Greece	58	21.3 (1988)	47.1	44.6	(Nisia)
Ireland	34	53.8	68.2	–	
Italy	36	57.0 (1988)	102.5	66.3	(Sicilia)
Luxembourg	100	42.7	123.7	–	
Netherlands	20	2.7	100.9	85.5	(Dost-Nederland)
Portugal	100	18.9	56.2	–	
Spain	58	28.0	75.4	59.1	(Sur)
UK	35	9.9	100.7	74.3	(N Ireland)

Notes
1. Expressed as the percentage of national workforce employed in areas eligible for regional aid.
2. £ per head of national population calculated using the 1989 Purchasing Power Parity Index for currency conversion.
3. Including former East Germany.
4. Excluding former East Germany.

Sources: Regional aid derived from *Journal of Regional Policy*, 12, 3–4, Dec., 1992; GDP – *Regional Trends*, 28, Table 2.1, p. 31, 1993.

surprisingly, there is a dichotomy, with some of the countries which may be expected to have most need of regional aid being least able to afford the expenditure – hence an EC role in the reallocation of national resources. Britain ranks around the middle of EC countries in terms of regional aid coverage and towards the lower end in terms of per capita expenditure on regional aid, although it should be noted that the difficulties of international expenditure comparisons are such that Table 4.5 is better seen as an indicator of relative national expenditure than as a precise guide to national differences. Note also that even in Denmark, with very low levels of current coverage and expenditure, former Development Region status (abolished in January 1991) may be used to justify ad hoc expenditure in support of potential major inward investment projects.

The second half of Table 4.5 gives some indication of the extent of national and regional disparities across Europe, using per capita Gross Domestic Product (GDP) as a measure of prosperity. Average national GDP/head varied from 24 per cent above the EC12 average in Luxembourg, to less than half the EC12 average in Greece. The final column of Table 4.5 gives the 1990 lowest regional GDP by country, and identifies the corresponding region. Regional EC disparities are substantially wider than national differences, with poorest region GDP as a share of the national average varying from 56 per cent in Italy to 95 per cent in Greece, implying that the extent of regional differences vary considerably across Europe. Taking poorest region GDP as a proportion of the national average is a crude indication of regional differences which would place the United Kingdom second (behind Italy) in an EC league table of regional disparities. However, if Northern Ireland is excluded on the grounds of its own special circumstances, the UK would move rapidly down the European league table of regional disparity on this measure. Moreover, in a 'Europe of the Regions', European regional differences may be much more important than national regional differences. For example, it may be little comfort to Greece that their regional differences are relatively narrow, when the Greek national average GDP was less than half the EC average.

4.6   REGIONAL ECONOMIC CHARACTERISTICS AND INWARD INVESTMENT

Whether in a UK or European context, various regional characteristics are likely to be seen as important by differing inward investors, according to their own requirements. We have already seen that regional financial incentives, operating through Regional Selective Assistance, can provide a significant capital subsidy to qualifying projects in Assisted Areas, and that, not surprisingly, the Assisted Areas have been major beneficiaries of the inward investment boom (see Chapter 3, especially Table 3.8). Similarly, different regions have had varying degrees of success in attracting overseas firms from particular source countries and into particular sectors. Welsh success in attracting Japanese investment, and Scottish success in attracting overseas producers of electronics are obvious examples. Less obvious have been the causes and effects of manufacturing intensity across regions, and its interaction with inward investment. Table 4.1 had earlier shown how the contribution of manufacturing to GDP varied between regions. This manufacturing share of regional GDP can now be seen as weakly associated with inward investment intensity. Whilst a full examination of the relationship between inward investment and other regional economic characteristics is the subject of the next chapter, Table 4.6 sets out some further dimensions of manufacturing intensity by region.

The table shows clearly the continued structural change away from manufacturing, with manufacturing's share of total UK employment falling from over 28 per cent to just 20 per cent in a decade. However, the decline in manufacturing's share of employment varied considerably by region. Whilst every region saw manufacturing's share of employment fall, the decline was greatest in the Midlands (both East and West) and in the North West, and least in Wales and East Anglia, both of which switched from less than the national average to more.

Figures for Gross Value Added per manufacturing employee (that is total revenue minus the value of bought-in materials and

Table 4.6   Regional manufacturing intensity, 1981 and 1991 (UK = 100)

	Manufacturing as share of employment		*Gross value added per person employed in manufacturing*	
	1981	*1991*	*1981*	*1990*
North	30.2	22.7	106.0	99.4
Yorks/Humber	31.4	23.8	91.7	93.4
East Midlands	36.3	27.1	87.5	88.5
East Anglia	27.2	22.4	106.0	102.0
South East	23.2	15.6	109.5	110.8
South West	25.7	18.2	103.0	93.4
West Midlands	39.9	29.2	88.5	88.1
North West	32.8	23.6	100.4	105.7
Wales	25.6	20.6	93.9	108.3
Scotland	25.4	18.1	106.7	106.0
N Ireland	23.3	17.2	90.5	86.0
UK	28.5	20.3	£10 027	£22 945

Sources: *Regional Trends*, NIERC, *Regional Economic Outlook*, 1993.

components), although slightly more dated, reveal a pattern that is in many ways surprising. Whilst higher levels of GVA/ employee can be anticipated for the South East, where relatively high earnings imply high capital to labour ratios, that GVA per employee should be substantially higher than the UK average in 1990 for Wales, Scotland and the North West is less obvious. Once more the relationship with inward investment is less than direct, since Wales and Scotland have earlier been identified as relatively most successful regions in attracting inward investment with the North West, Yorks/Humberside and the South East as least successful. Whilst each of the former had in 1990 a GVA/ employee in manufacturing in excess of the UK average, so to did two out of three of the latter.

The next table (Table 4.7) shows average earnings by region in 1992 relative to the UK average, both for manufacturing and for all industries and services. Once more earnings are highest in the

Table 4.7   Average British earnings, 1992 (GB = 100)

| | Manufacturing | | All industries and services | |
	Male	Female	Male	Female
North	96.3	93.3	92.4	91.5
Yorks/Humber	93.4	87.0	90.4	90.5
East Midlands	91.7	88.7	90.0	89.6
East Anglia	99.4	95.5	94.5	92.0
South East	114.7	121.3	115.2	115.0
South West	96.5	97.9	92.7	93.3
West Midlands	93.5	90.6	91.8	89.8
North West	98.1	94.8	94.1	92.9
Wales	90.5	90.9	88.0	90.7
Scotland	97.7	91.7	95.4	92.0
N Ireland	83.8	80.9	87.7	93.0

Sources: derived from *Regional Trends*, 28, 1993.

South East, followed by the South West and East Anglia, although, with the exception of Northern Ireland, manufacturing earnings are rather less regionally dispersed than are overall earnings. Once more the relationship between relative earnings and the regional distribution of FDI will be explored in the following chapter – for the moment it is sufficient to note that, excluding Northern Ireland, the regions with highest relative success in attracting FDI (Wales, the North, Scotland) had relative earnings that were well below the UK average – as did several regions (East Midlands, Yorks/Humberside) that have had markedly less success in attracting FDI. As we shall see, the role of earnings in the relative distribution of FDI is a complex matter.

Of rather more importance, to the indigenous as well as the inward investing firm, is the impact of earnings on unit labour costs via productivity. Traditionally, low relative wage regions have been associated with relatively low labour productivity, negating any regional wage cost advantages. Table 4.8 shows that the winning regions in FDI terms have been those in which pro-

Table 4.8   Productivity and unit labour costs in manufacturing, 1979, 1986 and 1991 (UK = 100)

	Productivity[1](GDP/ person)			Unit labour costs[2]		
	1979	1986	1991	1979	1986	1991
North	101.3	103.9	115.3	101.6	107.5	97.8
Yorks/Humber	93.1	96.7	93.5	102.1	103.6	99.8
East Midlands	92.3	90.9	92.6	103.4	104.2	102.3
East Anglia	104.4	102.5	103.3	95.3	95.0	100.6
South East	110.4	105.0	103.9	95.4	95.5	99.3
South West	100.4	96.7	90.8	100.6	111.5	109.4
West Midlands	90.4	91.3	93.7	106.3	100.4	103.4
North West	103.3	105.0	106.2	97.0	97.2	96.2
Wales	89.9	112.6	110.2	113.9	96.1	91.7
Scotland	100.9	99.8	99.7	98.3	102.2	99.4
N Ireland	81.4	84.0	83.5	109.7	104.9	106.3

Notes
1. Productivity is here defined as manufacturing GDP per person employed in manufacturing in the region, indexed to the UK average.
2. Unit labour cost is defined as average manufacturing earnings divided by average manufacturing GDP (output) per person employed, or the wage bill as a proportion of total output.

Source: Hill and Keegan (1993).

ductivity growth has interacted with relatively low earnings to push unit labour costs well below the UK average.

With the exception of the South East, which faces special constraints, especially in terms of land availability, the regions which have had least relative success in attracting inward investment projects and jobs have been those that experienced high relative unit labour costs, that is the South West, East Midlands and to a lesser extent West Midlands. Relatively high unit labour costs in the West Midlands have been somewhat offset by Assisted Area status and subsequent aid. Of the three regions of lowest unit labour costs in 1992, two (Wales and the North) have had most relative success in attracting new inward investment in recent years. This of course raises the familiar problem of what is the cause and consequence of new inward investment – have new projects been attracted by relatively low unit labour costs, or have they themselves forced unit labour costs downwards?

The final regional characteristic that may be expected to influence the location decision of the inward investor is the availability and rate of improvement of the transport infrastructure. As already noted, a regional manufacturing location is used as a springboard to market access in national and European terms: the inward investor is then crucially concerned with the nature of transport facilities locally, regionally and nationally, in terms of the ability and cost of moving inputs and outputs. The transport infrastructure is then a vital ingredient in the cost-minimising mix, with the impact of regional economic characteristics on production costs being offset or enhanced by the position of the particular site relative to transport facilities. In particular access to the road distribution network is a key. variable in securing access to national, and, via port facilities, international markets. There is little doubt that whilst other infrastructure dimensions such as rail, telecommunications and airport facilities are important, it is the changing state of the road (especially trunk-road) network that has most influence on the accessibility (and hence costs) of given manufacturing locations. Table 4.9 estimates the distribution of public expenditure on motorways and trunk roads (including new construction and improvements) by region from 1981/82 to 1990/91. Note the caveats at the bottom of the table. In aggregate terms public spending on improving and extending the major road network increased from £680m in 1981 to just over £1541m in 1990.

Not surprisingly given its size, the South East has taken the lion's share of road spending, although the South East's share, having been over 40 per cent in the first half of the decade, fell to between a quarter and a third in the later years of the 1980s. For the other regions some trends and constancies emerge, although the figures are susceptible to distortions because of particular

Table 4.9   Regional share of public spending on motorways and trunk roads (new plus improvements) 1981–90

| | Regional shares (% of Britain) | | | | | | | | | |
	81	*82*	*83*	*84*	*85*	*86*	*87*	*88*	*89*	*90*
North	5.5	4.5	2.3	2.2	1.6	2.1	5.8	4.5	5.2	3.6
Yorks/										
Humber	6.7	4.7	4.9	3.5	3.0	5.2	6.2	4.2	2.6	2.7
East Mids	4.0	3.0	3.6	6.3	6.0	5.1	4.8	7.8	7.6	9.9
South East	40.8	43.1	40.3	43.2	45.8	35.9	33.4	25.0	34.0	41.8
South West	4.2	5.1	7.1	5.0	4.3	7.0	10.8	11.0	8.0	7.7
West Mids	6.0	6.9	8.2	13.3	14.5	13.8	9.2	17.2	18.5	9.9
North West	10.6	8.3	6.9	4.7	3.7	5.6	5.0	7.8	5.4	6.1
Wales	11.5	13.0	16.3	10.6	8.8	12.4	12.9	12.8	8.9	9.1
Scotland	10.7	11.3	10.4	11.2	12.3	12.8	11.9	9.6	9.8	9.3
Britain £m	680.8	699.9	692.9	717.1	678.6	613.1	774.5	942.5	1151.1	1541.0

Notes   Figures for 1985 are estimated, as are underlying expenditure figures for Wales 1981–4 and Scotland 1981–90.

Source: Derived from *Transport Statistics, Great Britain*, various (London, HMSO).

major projects. Recall that the regions identified as having the highest relative success at attracting new inward investment in recent years have been Wales, Scotland and the North, with the North West, Yorks/Humberside and the South East seen as relatively least successful. Table 4.9 shows that each of the 'winning' regions in inward investment terms had disproportionately high shares of new road spending, with relatively less successful regions having declining shares of road spending. Notice that, with the exception of 1987, the improvement in West Midlands relative inward investment performance has been coterminous with its increasing share of major road spending in Britain.

Note also however, that Table 4.9 considers only improvements/extensions to the major road network. A region already well-served with motorways and trunk roads would require (and receive) relatively low levels and shares of new major road spending. Hence Table 4.9 can only be taken as an indicator of *changes* in relative road infrastructure, whereas any road infrastructure impact on new inward investment may be dominated by the previous stock of road networks.

Taken singly, relative earnings, productivities, unit labour costs, preferential assistance and infrastructure spending may offer partial explanation for the shifting distribution of inward investment in Britain over time and between regions. It remains an empirical question to determine the relative and joint impact of each on the changing pattern of new FDI between regions. Before moving on to consider the quantitative impact of each, it is useful to consider more explicitly, if briefly, the potential and actual relationship between inward investment and regional economic development.

4.7   REGIONAL ECONOMIC DEVELOPMENT AND INWARD INVESTMENT

The attraction of inward investment is readily perceived as a substantial benefit to nations, regions and localities. As noted earlier, a great deal of public effort and resources is expended on this, with inward investment seen as a vital ingredient in the promotion of regional economic development. Indeed there is hardly a local authority in the UK which does not have the attraction of foreign manufacturing investment as a major objective and commitment.

Yet even in regions identified as most successful in attracting new foreign firms, foreign-owned company employment accounts for well under a tenth of all employment, and often considerably less. What then is the impact of FDI on the local and regional economies and is the attraction of inward investment worthy of its assumed position at the centre of regional policy in Britain? More particularly, is the pursuit of foreign companies a cost-effective route to regional economic development, or would other policy options, such as greater support for indigenous firms, offer equivalent or improved value for money? Inevitably such economic questions are easier to raise than to answer.

The announcement, often by a politician, of some new inward investment project is normally qualified in terms of some substantial capital outlay and anticipated number of new jobs. These are the obvious direct consequences of the investment which, if subject to the conditions of Regional Selective Assistance, should be additional expenditure and jobs creating obvious and direct employment in the vicinity of the new manufacturing site. As noted earlier (Table 1.6), since 1984 the UK has attracted an average of over 300 new inward investment projects per year, bringing the promise of an annual addition of around 25 000 permanent new jobs. Many of these direct jobs have been relatively well-paid, involving work in capital-intensive and high technology industries that have been instrumental in increasing regional output and consequent incomes (see, for example, Morris, Munday and Wilkinson, 1994). Further direct effects include the boost to local labour and housing markets, as well as direct multiplier effects as additional incomes are spent in local markets (induced income effects – see, for example, Roberts, 1993).

Almost as important, in some locations, have been the indirect or second-round effects of the initial investment, as new firms seek local suppliers and buy-in other services, including engineering, marketing, legal, property and other professional services. Moreover, there is mounting evidence that these indirect effects increase over time, as the new inward investor takes time to acquire the information necessary to be able to substitute local for more distant sources, hence reducing transaction costs, and as new and existing suppliers take time to learn to meet the price and quality requirements and expectations of the newly arrived firm from overseas (see Hines, 1993). Indeed, recent estimates of the multiplier impact of inward investment in a particular region suggest that every direct job created can be associated with another 0.7 indirect jobs in a local supplier (either directly to the new manufacturer, or to some supplier to the new manufacturer, or to some supplier of the enhanced local workforce), vastly increasing the cost-effectiveness of attracting new inward investment (Hill and Roberts, 1993).

More generally, there is a widespread expectation that the new inward investor brings new trading opportunities to other firms and organisations in the region, and can help to diversify the regional manufacturing base, especially in aiding the replacement of heavier, traditional manufacturing industry by newer, lighter, higher value-added activities. Obvious examples include the Scottish and Welsh economies, where the run-down of traditional coal and steel sectors has been partially offset (at least in terms of aggregate output and employment) by the emergence of newer industries, even if these new industries have not generally provided job opportunities for redundant steelworkers or coal-miners. The importance of a diversified regional manufacturing base is clear in the regional response to a national recession – both Wales and Scotland appeared to weather the UK recession of the early 1990s rather better than that of the early 1980s (Northern Ireland Economic Research Centre, 1993). Part of the reason for this reduced sensitivity to the national economy is the higher export orientation of the inward investor, who typically sees a continental European market as at least as important as the domestic market. By the same token, an increased regional dependence on European Community markets may have adverse consequences if, for example, the rest of Europe were to lag behind Britain in recovery from recession.

The improved manufacturing competitiveness (in terms of unit labour costs) of these regions that had attracted disproportionately high shares of new inward investment has already been noted, alongside the difficulties of assigning causality. One obvious reason why new inward investment may contribute to lower unit labour costs is the tendency for the inward investor to employ relatively high levels of manufacturing capital, leading to high levels of gross value-added per employee and high rates of productivity (value of output per employee). Given that improved productivity is ultimately the key to high living standards, the attraction of inward investment offers a 'fast track' route to increased prosperity. By the same token it should be noted that the recent relative inward investment success of Wales, Scotland and the North has yet to be translated into obvious improvements in personal indicators of economic well-being (especially earnings and personal or household incomes – see Hill and Keegan, 1993).

If inward investment increases profitable trading opportunities, it should ultimately give a boost to 'entrepreneurship', possibly reflected in the relative growth of profits (as a share of GDP), self-employment and new firm formation. Some indications of the change in these variables over time by region is given by Table 4.10 which lists profits/surpluses as a share of GDP by region for 1981 and 1991, self-employment as a share of the workforce for 1981 and 1992, and the net annual average growth rate of the number of new companies, as measured by the levels of VAT registration over the 1981–91 period. Whilst there are obvious dangers in identifying each as a single measure of enterprise,

Table 4.10   Profits share of GDP, self-employment and VAT registration in UK regions[1]

	Profit/surpluses as share of GDP (%)		Self-employed as share of workforce (%)		Annual/average growth rate in VAT registration[2], 1981–91
	1981	1991	1981	1992	
North	15.1	15.0	6.0	8.3	1.80
Yorks/Humber	14.5	14.6	7.3	10.1	1.94
East Midlands	12.9	13.6	8.2	10.4	2.43
East Anglia	13.5	11.1	10.5	13.6	2.51
South East	11.1	9.4	8.2	11.3	3.36
South West	12.1	9.6	12.3	12.7	2.47
West Midlands	12.2	13.0	6.8	9.7	2.21
North West	14.8	14.3	7.1	9.7	1.78
Wales	13.4	16.4	9.6	13.7	1.73
Scotland	14.5	12.2	6.1	9.4	2.06
UK	12.7	12.9	8.0	10.8	2.53

Notes
1. Table excludes Northern Ireland.
2. Adjusted for the impact of budget changes.

Source: Taken or derived from *Regional Trends*, various.

taken together they may offer some pointers to a tenuous relationship between success at attracting new FDI and entrepreneurship.

The national share of profits in GDP was broadly comparable in 1981 and 1991, presumably reflecting the similar position of each year in the economic cycle (that is, each was a recession year). In 1981, regions with highest profit shares in GDP were the North, North West, Scotland and Yorks/Humberside, with the South East having lowest profit share. By 1991 Wales had moved to highest profit share, as well as highest relative success in attracting inward investment, although followed in terms of profit share (but not relative inward investment success) by Yorks/Humberside and the North West. Similarly, whilst Wales and Scotland experienced the highest percentage increases in self-employment as a share of the workforce between 1981 and 1992, they were closely followed by the South East and East Anglia, areas of relatively low success in attracting new inward investment. Hence the evidence as far as inward investment, self-employment and profits as a share of GDP is concerned is far from clear. Moreover, examination of the growth rate of new firms (as measured by net VAT registrations), shows if anything a negative correlation with relative inward investment success, with regions of least relative inward investment success (South East, East Anglia and South West) experienceing highest growth rates in VAT registration, whilst the best performing regions in attracting inward investment (Wales, Scotland and the North) were amongst the lowest in terms of VAT registration growth rates.

Overall, if there is an association between relative success at attracting inward investment and rough and ready indicators of entrepreneurship, then neither the nature of the association nor the direction of causation is clear.

Finally, further benefits of inward investment to regional economic development include intangibles such as the stimulus of new management styles and ideas, as well as the opportunity for technology transfer, amply evidenced by emerging relationships between inward investors and their suppliers (Morris, Munday and Wilkinson, 1993).

4.8 CONCLUSIONS

There is little doubt about the potential for new inward investment to act as a stimulus to local and regional economic development, with indirect or multiplier effects being potentially as important as the initial impacts of new capital spending and new jobs. The attraction of inward investment is now at the forefront of regional economic policy in Britain, as elsewhere in Europe. Yet there are justifiable concerns about the abilities of regional economies to translate this stimulus into economic growth, which then permeates the regional economic fabric and enhances mutual economic well-being in the regions. At the same time the position of inward investment as the remaining plank of regional policy raises questions about the desirability of having regions compete against each other, as well as against other European regions, in some sort of 'beauty' parade for the inward investor. In addition, fears remain about the substitution of a European regional policy for any serious national regional policy in the UK.

References

Griffiths, A. and Wall, S. (1989), *Applied Economics: An Introductory Course*, Harlow: Longman.

Hardwick, P., Khan, B. and Langmead, J. (1990), *An Introduction to Modern Economics*, Harlow: Longman.

Hill, S. and Keegan, J. (1993), *Made in Wales: Relative Manufacturing Performance*, Cardiff: CBI Wales.

Hill, S. and Minford, P. (1993), 'Regional Analysis', *Welsh Economic Review*, 6, 1, Spring, 3–4.

Hill, S. and Roberts, A. (1993), 'Input–Output Analysis and the Welsh Economy', *Welsh Economic Review*, 6, 1, Spring, 50–56.

Hines, P. (1993), 'The Supplier Initiative', *Welsh Economic Review*, Special Issue on Inward Investment, Institute of Welsh Affairs, June, 38.

Morris, J. (1987), 'Industrial Restructuring, Foreign Direct Investment and Uneven Developments: the Case of Wales', *Environment and Planning A, 19*, 205–44.

Morris, J., Munday, M. and Wilkinson, B. (1993), *Working for the Japanese*, London: Athlone.

Northern Ireland Economic Research Centre (1992), *Regional Economic Outlook*, OEF: NIERC.

Northern Ireland Economic Research Centre (1993), *Regional Economic Outlook*, OEF: NIERC.

Roberts, A. (1993), 'The Causes and Consequences of Inward Investment in Wales', *Contemporary Wales*, forthcoming.

5 The Determinants of the Regional Distribution of Foreign Direct Investment

5.1 INTRODUCTION

Earlier chapters noted the increasingly active participation of the UK in world flows of direct investment, and particularly with respect to inward investment, alongside the shifting UK regional pattern of this investment. The purpose of this chapter is to advance some simple hypotheses to explain the changing behaviour of the new inward investor with regard to regional location, and to show how these hypotheses can be empirically defined and then tested. Despite the numerous and sometimes severe nature of the theoretical and empirical problems encountered, this chapter will show that variation in the UK distribution of new FDI can be largely explained in terms of relatively few regional economic characteristics. The relationship between the regional pattern of inward investment and these economic characteristics is consistent with a number of models of MNE behaviour including the preferred simple explanation that the new foreign investor chooses a UK regional location in order to minimise the relevant costs of production whilst securing access to adjacent national and international markets. The policy implications that stem from this simple model and its verification are many and substantial. For example, the sectoral marketing and employment policies of the new inward investor will largely determine the mix of regional characteristics that are necessary in order to minimise production costs, including transport costs, and will therefore according to this model, influence regional location. Hence particular regions will not only attract differing shares of inward investment according to their regional characteristics, but the very nature of the inward investors attracted will reflect the particular mix of economic characteristics that the region can offer.

This chapter will proceed by briefly reviewing the current state of theoretical explanations of MNE behaviour, before advancing the central hypotheses that make up the core of this treatment. The next section will outline the nature and anticipated influence of the very economic characteristics that are expected to be influential determinants of FDI regional location. Some discussion of the difficulties of relating actual regional data to the defined theoretical variables will ensue. This is a topic that re-emerges in the next section which seeks to regionally define and measure inward investment success that is the dependent variables of this study.

Whilst detailed regional figures for each dependent and independent variables are relegated to the data appendix to this chapter the text will include a brief analysis of parameter changes over time.

The next section will outline the estimation procedure, including the econometric problems encountered in the complex procedures of pooled data analysis, ie. the composite treatment of cross-sectional (across UK regions) data over time. Tests for stability will measure the appropriateness of adapted procedures. The full empirical results of this analysis will follow, including the detailed description of what those results mean and their implications. This will lead to the concluding section, drawing together the previous section, and assessing the economic and policy implications of these results.

The basic justification for this research and analysis is the assertion that by its very nature inward investment is somehow different from indigenous investment, and hence has both different attractions and different implications, particularly for regional economic development (see section 4.6 above). This differential nature has long been recognised: for example, McDermott (1977) argued that understanding the locational choices of foreign-owned enterprise was essential to assessment of the impact of FDI, whilst Yannopoulos and Dunning (1976) were amongst the first to recognise the developmental implication of the differences between indigenous and overseas investors. These differences are fully explored in the text of Hood and Young (1979). The nature of these differences include size (in terms of sales or employment), working practices and organisation technology (including capital investments) as well as the complex pattern of buyer/supplier relationships. These differences have direct effects on the regional developmental implications of new investments: for example if low wages were the primary attraction to foreign-owned manufacturing capital, particular kinds of labour intensive, assembly-type operations would be enticed, limiting the regional economic impact of this investment.

5.2   THEORIES OF LOCATIONAL CHOICE

Chapter 2 provided a review of the motives for FDI, including notions of capital adequacy and the idea of ownership-advantage, that is, that the MNE has some intrinsic competitive advantage that can be fully exploited by the transfer of manufacturing facilities to an overseas market. The advantages could include expertise in production techniques or in marketing product developments that allow differentiation or favoured access to some essential markets, materials or components. This ownership advantage approach was further developed by combination with theories of oligopolistic market structure, highlighting the notion of competitive advantage in a restricted market through economies of scale and scope and the greater ability to innovate in products, production techniques or in marketing.

The ownership-advantage approach can be contrasted with the development of theory explaining the existence of the MNE through the idea of the internalisation of transactions cost, an idea first put forward by Coase (1937), but introduced into a theory of multinational enterprise by economists Buckley and Casson (1976). In particular, Buckley and Casson argued that multinationals developed because of market failure, especially the high transactions costs involved in the international transfer and exploitation of knowledge.

These contrasting approaches soon found integration in the 'eclectic' paradigm advanced by John Dunning in 1976, subsequently revised and reviewed in 1991. Dunning showed that the foreign firm must have some competitive advantage allowing it to overcome the extra costs of producing abroad, and that producing abroad must be more profitable than either licensing or exporting. If these conditions are not met the form of overseas investment is likely to involve joint ventures or portfolio investment, rather than direct investment.

One complementary approach is the 'product life cycle' hypothesis advanced by Vernon (1971) to suggest that MNE's developed in order to seize new market and marketing opportunities abroad, as domestic markets entered the mature low growth phase of product development.

Rather more radical was the New International Division of Labour Model, which saw Foreign Direct Investment as the manifestation of the need to maximise profit from the partial redistribution of functions so that productive activity was placed in its most appropriate (that is, least-cost) location in order to meet global market demand whilst responding to local economic conditions. Such an approach would point, for example, to US direct investment in Puerto Rico, or at Japanese investment in Ireland, as a consequence of cost-minimisation whilst securing tariff-free market access (Schoenberger, 1988).

Whilst these theories of the causes and motivations of foreign direct investment flow are of substantial intrinsic interest to the analyst concerned with foreign firm location-decisions, they cast relatively little light on either the nature of that locational choice or its impact on regional distributions. Indeed empirical analysis of the distribution of foreign direct investment between nations and regions has tended to be data-led rather than theory-driven (see Coughlin *et al.*, 1991 and Glickman and Woodward, 1988). Such studies have revealed a great deal about the nature of local economic conditions that inward investors appear to find attractive. McConnell (1980) suggested that by 'following the leader' overseas firms could minimise both the risk of subsequent failure and the cost of locational search, implying that the existing stock of foreign direct investment will act as a magnet to further investment. The evidence of a shifting pattern of new inward investment in the UK away from traditional core areas to new peripheral locations may suggest that the days of such agglomeration impact are over, with overseas firms now expecting a substantial return on locational search activity.

Not surprisingly, the focus of academic research on the regional location of inward investment has been on the distribution of FDI between American states. Little (1978) was amongst the first to use regression analysis to show that the state distribution of FDI was more related to labour market conditions and transport infrastructure than the comparable distribution of indigenous investments. Glickman and Woodward (1988) used a similar methodology to show how the location of foreign-owned manufacturing plants could be related to cost-variables such as energy costs, the condition of local labour markets and essential local infrastructure. More recently, Bagchi-Sen and Wheeler (1989) related foreign service-sector investment in the US to population size and growth rates alongside per-capita consumer retail spending.

The most recent fashion for empirical analysis of state locational choice in the US has been for Conditional-Logit models. Luger and Shetty (1985) looked at new foreign-owned plant location between US states for the period 1979–83 to conclude that market size, promotional spending, and local wage rates were each significant influences on site choice. Coughlin *et al.* (1991) examined manufacturing investment by foreign companies between 1981 and 1983 across US states to deduce that market size, the quality of transport infrastructure and promotional spending, as well as local labour variables, such as the rate of unionisation and the local unemployment rate, were positively related to the likelihood of a particular state being chosen as a location whilst such choice was negatively related to the local wage rate.

Woodward (1992) analysed locational choice amongst US states of Japanese manufacturing investors over a ten year period (1980–89). Whilst his general results were mixed, a positive and significant relationship between the probability of choice and market size was found, as was a negative relationship to the level of local unionisation. Finally, Freidman *et al.* (1992) relate new foreign manufacturing investment across US states between 1977 and 1988 to a range of local economic characteristics to find a positive relationship between the chance of a particular state being chosen and market size, the level of unionisation, promotional spending, local unemployment rates, labour productivity and a transportation variable (actually a dummy variable signifying state access to port facilities), and a negative relationship to the level of local taxes and relative wage rates.

The common feature of this American evidence is the consensus that the distribution of new inward investment across US states is influenced by relative market size, manufacturing wage rates, transport infrastructures and state promotional expenditure designed to attract new inward investment.

Hence, Freidman *et al.* summarise the current state of evidence from the US as showing that access to domestic (US) markets as well as access to foreign markets is important to foreign-owned manufacturing location. Hence seaboard states with both large, local markets, and good international port facilities have been the primary locations for new inward investors (that is, the North East and Mid-Pacific states). However manufacturing wages and labour productivity were also influential, as was state promotional activity.

Evidence from the UK and the rest of Europe is neither as plentiful, nor typically, as recent. European studies have tended to concentrate on the flow of foreign capital between nations rather than within regions of particular nations (see, for example, Grubaugh, 1987, Taylor and Thrift, 1982). However, Culem (1988) reviews the impact of locational characteristics on the distribution of FDI between European countries, whilst O'Sullivan (1985) examines the relationship between host country parameters and the level of direct investment into Ireland. Rather earlier Blackbourne (1978) had noted the concentration of foreign-owned manufacturing within core regions of the developed economies, whilst Dicken and Lloyd (1976) had emphasised the tendency of FDI to locate in the South East of England. McDermott (1977) was amongst the first to suggest a shift in the new investment decisions of overseas companies towards the periphery (especially to the Assisted Areas), whilst Watts (1982) noted a reluctance for new German investors to site between core and peripheral regions of the UK. More recently Hill and Munday (1991) used regression analysis to relate the level and share of new inward investment to a particular UK region (Wales). They found that the level of new capital/direct investment into Wales from overseas was negatively related to the Wales/UK earnings ratio and positively related to the level of Regional Preferential Assistance into Wales. The Welsh share of new UK inward investment was negatively related to the Wales/ UK earnings ratio and positively related to the Welsh share of both Preferential Assistance and infrastructure spending. This analysis was later extended (Hill and Munday, 1992) to the distribution of new inward investment across UK regions to show that relative regional shares were influenced by shares of preferential assistance, relative earnings and share of new road spending. It is this later work that will be developed and extended here. The central message of this analysis will be that new inward investors entering the UK choose a regional location that minimises the relevant costs of production whilst securing access to national and international markets, particularly through the trunk road network.

5.3   MEASUREMENT AND METHOD

The distribution of inward investment across UK regions was the subject of Chapter 3, which defined and examined the relative success of different regions by reference to data on new projects and jobs collected by the Invest in Britain Bureau (IBB). The difficulties of collecting and interpreting these data were noted in Chapter 3, which then used these data together with information from the Census of Employment to define an index of relative performance in attracting inward investment as:

$$RA = \frac{\text{Region A share of UK new inward investment projects (jobs)}}{\text{Region A share of national employment}}$$

These defined indices then formed the basis for Tables 3.7 and 3.8, which clearly showed the relative success of Wales, Scotland the North and to a lesser extent the West Midlands, in attracting new projects and jobs, and the relative lack of success of the South East, Yorkshire/Humberside, South West and the East Midlands on the same criteria. Table 5.1 is the 'league' table of defined relative inward investment performance of the regions, averaged over the ten year period 1982–91.

The relative performance index by region over ten years (1982–91) provides ninety observations ranging from 0.06 (that is, the South East gained just 6 per cent of its UK share of employment in inward investment projects in 1990) to 6.50 (Wales receiving six and a half times her share of UK employment in inward investment associated jobs in 1991). The objective of explaining the regional distribution of inward investment

Table 5.1   Relative inward investment performance, 1982–91

Region	Project index	Region	Job index
Wales	3.73	Wales	3.73
North	2.00	Scotland	2.62
Scotland	1.72	North	2.25
W Midlands	1.67	W Midlands	1.51
North West	1.13	E Midlands	0.75
E Midlands	0.69	North West	0.73
Yorks/Humberside	0.62	South West	0.70
South East	0.44	Yorks/Humberside	0.52
South West	0.43	South East	0.30

Note: Table 3.7 dealt with the period 1982–1992, whilst the empirical analysis covers 1982–1991; thus these league table numbers are slightly different from those in Table 3.8.

Source: adapted from Table 3.7.

across the UK then narrows to that of explaining the pattern of defined relative success (Appendix 5A), which then provides the dependent variables for this analysis.

The methodological approach adopted was to seek to explain the variations in this relative index via a series of host region characteristics that are consistent with the cost-minimisation/ adjacent market access hypotheses: that is:

RA = f (relative cost-influencing/access characteristics of region A)

This then left two related methodological issues – the identification of host region characteristics likely to be important to either production costs or market access, and the estimation of a precise relationship between the dependent variables and host-region variables. The latter problem was addressed through the method of least squares linear regression (that is, the estimating of the straight-line relationship of best-fit), whilst the former issue will be dealt with in the next section. However, the form of the data (nine regions over ten years) meant the pooling of cross-section and time series observations, a process that makes explicit assumptions about the nature of regional and time-trend influences, and which raises the potential problem of heteroscedasticity and the possibility that differences between modelled and actual dependent variables were related to either time-trend or regional influences. Fortunately, tests of stability, in particular the estimation of a model including a full set of regional and time-trend variables, offered little improvement in explanatory power. Hence the adopted method of regressing the defined relative index against a set of independent variables chosen to reflect the central hypotheses was appropriate (see Hill and Munday, 1992).

5.4   INFLUENCES ON THE REGIONAL DISTRIBUTION OF FDI

The assumed objective of the new inward investor choosing a UK regional location, will be to site so as to minimise production costs whilst securing market access. The cost of producing in a particular location will be governed by a combined set of company-specific and locational variables, including the production of inputs and their cost at the specific location.

The general locational characteristics that can be expected to influence costs were considered in Chapter 4 and above. As noted earlier, the US consensus points to local market size, manufacturing wages, infrastructure and state promotional spending as primary influences on the state distribution of new inward investment. UK evidence has pointed to the labour market and financial assistance as characteristics with sufficient variation to influence regional locations. One further influence posited here is improvements in the transport infrastructure which reduce transport costs and/or improve access to national and international markets.

The regional/locational labour market has a whole series of dimensions, that may influence labour costs and hence the costs of production. Dimensions measured in other empirical investigations include the level of unionisation, wage rates, unemployment levels and productivity (see, for example, Freidman *et al.*, 1992). Unfortunately, most of these characteristics are closely correlated with each other, leading to severe estimation problems. Essentially what is required is some summary characteristic which adequately reflects regional variations in labour market conditions. An ideal index would be unit labour costs, taking account of variations in both regional wage rates and productivity differences and reflecting the regions occupational and industry mix. Unfortunately such an index is not yet available on a consistent basis across regions, although some preliminary steps have been taken (see Hill and Keegan, 1993). The regional labour market variables used in this analysis were wage rate and unemployment rates, each defined relative to the UK average. Chapter 4 has already shown that there are substantial regional variations in wages and unemployment levels across the UK. In particular, earnings in peripheral areas are traditionally lower than in the tighter (at least until recently) labour markets of the South East. Given that wage bills are typically a substantial proportion of total operating costs, low relative wages will be a significant inducement to peripheral location. Therefore it was anticipated that regional shares of new inward investment would be negatively related to relative wage levels (that is, relatively high wages would be associated with relatively low levels of new inward investment).

There is a wealth of published data relating to regional wage levels, including average earnings overall and by sector, by gender, by occupation, by full/part-time etc. Hence there is some difficulty in defining regional wage levels in a manner that captures the wage level influence on inward investment. One obvious choice was that of manufacturing rather than overall wages, since most of the foreign direct investment captured by the relative performance index is in manufacturing industry. However, this still left a division by gender/occupation/working time. Ultimately the procedure adopted was to use New Earnings Survey data on total wage bills divided by the total number of full-time equivalent employees, in order to capture the increasing influence in the new inward investors workforce of employment other than that of the traditional male manual full-time employees. Conveniently, this data manipulation is performed by the Northern Ireland Economic Research Centre/Oxford Economic Forecasting in their periodic regional review (see for example, Northern Ireland Economic Research Centre, 1993). Data Appendix 5B lists the full data-set of average manufacturing earnings relative to the UK average (RME) for the defined regions between 1981 and 1990.

Appendix 5B presents a number of surprises as far as relative earnings are concerned, particularly when contrasted with Table 4.3 in the previous chapter which listed overall gross weekly average earnings for UK regions in 1981 and 1991. Differences between Appendix 5B and Table 4.3 are remarkable, since the latter shows Wales, the North and Scotland as relatively low earnings areas whilst Appendix 5B shows the opposite. Remember, however, that Appendix 5B refers to average manufacturing earnings, whilst Table 4.3 was for overall earnings, that is including the much larger service sector (see Table 4.8). Relatively high manufacturing earnings for the North, Wales and Scotland, particularly for the early 1980s, reflected the dominance of manu-facturing industry in these areas of traditionally high-paid/high-skill male jobs in heavy industries such as metal manufacturing or mechanical engineering. Note that for both Wales and Scotland relative manufacturing earnings have declined over the decade to 1990 as traditional jobs were largely replaced by newer light engineering/electronics jobs (often for female workers).

The other dimension of UK regional labour markets with which a relationship to relative inward investment success was sought was the regional unemployment rate. However, this raised two difficulties. The first was the strong negative correlation between regional unemployment and relative manufacturing earnings so that when both were included in the estimation pro-cess their combined effect was divided in some arbitrary way. The usual tests of statistical significance provided empirical jus-tification for the use of relative manufacturing earnings. The sec-ond justification for not using regional unemployment as an anticipated positive influence on new inward investment was the mounting evidence that the new inward investor typically took very few workers from the unemployment register directly, although of course there are likely to be indirect effects on local unemployment stemming from new inward investment (see, for example, Morris *et al.*, 1993).

The second posited influence on regional location under the cost-minimisation/market access paradigm is the availability of financial assistance from government. As noted earlier various regions have available a wide range of local, regional and national incentives to the new manufacturing investor from over-seas (or indeed, to indigenous investors). The general form of this assistance is a capital grant as some proportion of eligible capital expenditure, although the specific form and nature of this grant has varied by location and through time, with a general UK trend towards discretionary lower-level aid since the early 1990s. The specific incentive variable measured in this analysis is relative Regional Preferential Assistance using data published on an annual basis by the Central Statistics Office. Once more the definition adopted is a relative one that is indexed to the regions' employment size. More specifically, the variable RPA measures the regions share of total UK Regional Preferential Assistance spending, standardised for unequal regional size by dividing by regional shares of UK employment. Appendix 5C tabulates resulting values for the RPA variable. Whilst Table 4.6 earlier had set out Regional Preferential Assistance expenditure by region in £m for 1984/85 to 1991/2, Appendix 5C translates this spending into relative shares for calendar years, once more standardised by division according to employment shares. Not surprisingly given the Assisted Areas map for the period, the South East including East Anglia received no regional aid, whilst the South West, East and West Midlands, received very small amounts of aid in relation to their size, (although note the increasing West Midlands index after 1984). Once more it is Wales, Scotland and the North who have received disproportionately high shares of RPA in relation to their size, with Wales in particular consistently receiving a share of UK RPA well over four times her share of UK employment. As will be seen relative shares of RPA can be positively associated with high relative shares of new inward investment. Note that since new inward investment data refer to announcements, that is planned and anticipated projects and jobs, whilst RPA refers to actual spending in a period, any element of double counting is avoided. High RPA in a given year is not the consequence of high inward investment as measured in that year.

The final part of the inward investment paradigm involves access to national and international markets. That the upsurge of inward investment into the UK (and some other parts of Europe) coincided with the planning and introduction of the Single European market is well-known (see for example Hill and Munday, 1993). Moreover American evidence already cited has pointed to the importance of both local market access and access to international port facilities. An ideal index of market access would include some indication of the size (and growth) of local markets, the state (and improvements) of road, rail and air travel facilities as well as some indication of access to sea ports. Given the absence of such an indicator on a regional basis, a proxy indicator is used: that is, regional spending on the extension and improvement of the motorway/trunk road network. High levels (and shares) of regional spending on trunk road improvements is then used as an (imperfect) indicator of market access, reflecting the road distribution networks importance in both the distribution of output and the ease of input supply. Even the most casual of anecdotal observation is sufficient to note the tendency of the new inward investor to locate alongside the major trunk road/ motorway networks – obvious examples include Honda at Swindon, Toyota at Derby and Deeside, Kodak at Carlisle, Bosch at Pencoed and Hewlett Packard at Bristol and Reading. More systematically, the variable INF measures the regional share of UK spending on motorways and trunk road improvements, standardised once more through division by regional shares of UK employment. Somewhat surprisingly there are some data difficulties in estimating regional spending on the major road network on a consistent basis. Appendix 5D provides best estimates on a commonsense basis. According to Appendix 5D, there has been a considerable variation in relative shares of trunk road spending with only Wales and Scotland consistently receiving greater shares of UK road spending than their share of employment, presumably reflecting the on-going investments in the M4/A55 coastal routes in Wales, and extensions to the M74, south of Glasgow, in Scotland. Of the other regions the South East, East and West Midlands and the North have relative shares of road spending which have fluctuated around their shares of UK employment, whilst Yorks/Humberside and the North West have consistently received shares of UK road spending that are well below their respective shares of UK employment.

5.5   RESULTS

Recall that the basic methodology adopted was to regress the independent variables (relative inward investment performance in terms of projects and associated jobs) on the three independent variables measuring relative manufacturing earnings, regional preferential assistance and infrastructure improvements. The pooled sample of data provided 90 observations, for each variable; that is, nine regions over ten years (1982–91). However the independent variables were each lagged one-year to take account of the presumption that current inward investment decisions would be made on the basis of best-available information: that is, that for the previous year. Various lag structures were attempted with no empirical improvement to this basic model. Such a procedure has the added advantage of eliminating any potential endogeneity from the independent variables.

The intrinsic difficulty of comparing economic variables across regions of unequal size was overcome by the process of standardisation, that is, by relating the relevant variable to its UK equivalent. In other words the inward investment performance indicator (regions share of new projects or jobs) was divided by the regions share of UK employment thus defining an index with a UK standard value of unity. Each of the independent *expenditure* variables was adjusted in the same way (that is, by standardising shares of UK assistance or road spending by dividing through by shares of UK employment) whilst average manufacturing earnings by region was measured relative to the UK average.

Estimation of the simple straight line as a functional form offered both theoretical and practical benefits. The independent variables influencing inward investment were expected to have additive impact, whilst estimation using more complex functions offered no empirical advantage in terms of explanatory power. The basic equation estimated was then:

$$R/Y = a + b_1 (X_1/Y) + b_2 (X_2/Y) + b_3 X_3$$

where R = regional share of inward investment projects (or jobs)

X_1 = regional share of UK preferential assistance

X_2 = regional share of UK trunk road spending

X_3 = ratio of regional to UK average manufacturing earnings

Y = regional share of UK employment

with the minimising production cost/market access paradigm implying that:

$$b_1, b_2 > 0$$
$$b_3 \quad < 0$$

Hill and Munday (1992) show that this formulation is equivalent to assuming that in the absence of other influences, the regional distribution of new FDI would be uniform, or more specifically proportional to regional size as measured by employment. This assumption then provides the basis for empirical investigation, and represents an attempt to relate deviations in regional shares from this assumed uniform pattern to the identified product cost/market access variables. The basic empirical results of the estimation procedure are given in Table 5.2.

These results are a substantial improvement upon those of Hill and Munday (1992), in the sense of covering more data, having better defined (and hence more significant) independent variables and in achieving greater explanatory power.

Equation 1 explains two-thirds of the total variation in the relative regional inward investment performance index in relation to new inward investment jobs, with relative regional performance being positively associated with relative share of infrastructure

Table 5.2 Relative job/project performance in attracting new inward investment

---

1. Jobs =   4.604 + 0.583 RPA − 4.420 RME + 0.332 INF
   (t statistics)   (2.80)   (8.43)   (2.71)   (2.23)

   $R_2 = 0.67$ $F(3,86) = 60.05$

2. Projects =   3.465 + 0.456 RPA − 3.312 RME + 0.473 INF
   (t statistics)   (2.83)   (8.85)   (2.72)   (4.36)

   $R_2 = 0.74$ $F(3,86) = 85.33$

---

and regional aid spending (as defined), and negatively related to the relative manufacturing wage. According to equation 1, relative inward investment performance in terms of jobs is more sensitive to regional aid than to infrastructure spending. At the same time, increases in the relative manufacturing earnings would reduce regional relative success at attracting new jobs from inward investment. If, for a hypothetical region, the share of inward investment new jobs in any period exactly matched its share of UK employment then the proportionate impact of a given increase in relative manufacturing wage would be over four times the proportionate relative wage change; that is, inward investment new job share to a region is very sensitive to relative manufacturing wages.

Equation 2 provides an even better fit to the observations, with variations in the three independent variables being associated with almost three-quarters of the total variation in relative regional shares of new inward investment projects over the nine regions over ten years. This is a very close fit for this type of empirical investigation. Each of the estimated coefficients has the anticipated sign and is significantly different from zero. In other words relative regional success at attracting new inward investment projects can be shown to be negatively related to relative manufacturing earnings and positively related to shares of spending on regional aid and road infrastructure improvements. Relative project share was equally sensitive to shares of regional aid and road transport spending, and not surprisingly, less sensitive than job share to relative manufacturing earnings.

Recall that equation 1 and 2 represent pooled, time-series and cross-sectional data, and that the estimation procedure implicitly assumes that regional and time-period influences are negligible. In particular, equations 1 and 2 represent 'restricted' regression equations with the implicit restrictions that coefficients for time-period and regional influence variables were not significantly different from zero. This was tested explicitly by the definition of a full model including dummy variables for each time period (minus one) and for each region (minus one). This model was then estimated, with results compared to the initial (restricted) model to see if the index of regional and time dummies added significantly to the explanatory power. The model for jobs revealed no evidence of time period or regional influences thereby justifying the pooled data procedure, whilst the model for projects showed some signs of weak regional influences, and must therefore be treated with caution. Neither model showed any evidence of heteroscedasticity.

There are some remaining difficulties associated with the interpretation of equations 1 and 2. In particular both equations include both a capital subsidy variable (RPA) and a labour cost variable (RME). A capital subsidy can be expected to attract capital-intensive firms, whilst low relative manufacturing earnings could be expected to be associated with the attraction of labour-intensive firms. Hence high levels of capital subsidy could be associated with relatively high project shares whilst low relative manufacturing earnings could be associated with high relative job share for new inward investment. Hill and Munday (1992) suggest that in practice both effects would combine, since regions of low relative earnings could be expected to have high relative shares of regional aid (although note the evidence of Appendices 5B and 5C).

5.6   CONCLUSIONS

The purpose of this chapter was to identify the determinants of recent relative regional success at attracting new inward investment. The procedure adopted has been necessarily complex, with plenty of conditionalities and assumption. However, the central message is clear – regions that have performed best in attracting recent inward investment have been those able to offer highest shares of UK regional aid, highest shares of new road spending and low or declining levels of manufacturing earnings, each defined relative to the UK.

The policy implications are equally clear: there is little regions can do about relative manufacturing earnings in the short term, but shares of regional aid spending and shares of road-building expenditure are under political as well as economic influence. For example the recent re-drawing of the Assisted Areas map is an obvious case of political intervention. By including new Assisted Areas in the South East and South West, politicians will have had a direct bearing on the future location of new inward investment projects and jobs. Whether such intervention is justified in the light of the continuing regional economic disparities identified in Chapter 4 is another matter.

Throughout the decade under consideration, Wales and Scotland have each experienced disproportionately high shares of new inward investment. The evidence of Appendices 5A–D, as well as estimated equations 1 and 2, demonstrate clearly that this relative success can be related to the success of the regions in achieving disproportionately high shares of UK regional aid and new road spending, alongside levels of manufacturing earnings that have declined relative to the UK average. The Northern region has had a slightly different experience with relatively high manufacturing earnings and relatively low share of road spending being more than compensated by relatively high levels of regional assistance (averaging close to four times the regions share of UK employment over the decade).

Meanwhile regions of low relative success at attracting new inward investment (the South East, South West, Yorkshire/Humberside) have had low share of trunk road spending and regional aid. For other regions, inward investment influencing variables have offset or cancelled each other with for example the North West's relatively high share of regional aid being offset by low (and generally declining) share of trunk road spending.

The next chapter will examine in more detail the implications of this analysis, and will develop the empirical results, with some attempt to apply the general model to the particular experience of regions. The ultimate conclusion of the current evidence is however crystal-clear – the changing regional distribution of new inward investment over the past decade can be largely explained by just three regional economic characteristics – the regions' share of

UK regional aid and road infrastructure spending, and the regions' average manufacturing earnings relative to the UK average.

References

Bagchi-Sen, S. and Wheeler, J. O. (1989), 'A Spatial and Temporal Model of FDI in the US', *Economic Geography*, 65, 2, 113–29.

Blackbourne, A. (1978), 'Multinational Enterprise and Regional Development: A Comment', *Regional Studies*, 12, 125–7.

Buckley, P. J. and Casson, M. (1976), *The Future of the Multinational Enterprise* (2nd edn, 1991) London: Macmillan.

Coase, R. M. (1937), The Nature of the Firm, *Economica*, 4, 386–405.

Coughlin, C. C., Terza, J .V. and Arrundee, V. (1991), 'State Characteristics and the Location of Foreign Direct Investment Within the United States', *Review of Economics and Statistics*, 54, 440–49.

Culem, C. (1988), 'The Locational Determinants of Direct Investment Among Industrialised Countries', *European Economic Review*, 32, 885–904.

Dicken, P. and Lloyd, P. (1976), 'Geographical Perspectives on United States Investment in the UK', *Environment and Planning*, A 8, 685–705.

Dunning, J. H. (1976), 'Trade, Location of Economic Activity and the Multinational Enterprise: A Search for an Eclectic Approach', University of Reading Discussion Papers in International Investment and Business Studies, no. 29.

Dunning, J. H. (1991), The 'Eclectic Paradigm of International Production', in C. W. Pitelis and R. Sugden (eds), *The Nature of the Transnational Firm*, London: Routledge.

Freidman, J., Gerlowski, D. A. and Silberman, J. (1992), 'What Attracts Foreign Multinational Corporations? Evidence of Branch Plant Location in the United States', *Journal of Regional Science*, vol. 32, 4, 403–18.

Glickman, N. J. and Woodward, D. P. (1988), 'The Location of Foreign Direct Investment in the United States: Patterns and Determinants', *International Regional Science Review*, 11, 131–54.

Grubaugh, N. (1987), 'The Determinants of Foreign Direct Investment', *Review of Economics and Statistics*, 69, 149–52.

Hill, S. and Keegan, J. (1993), 'Relative Regional Manufacturing Performance', Regional Science Association, British Section, Annual Conference, Nottingham, September.

Hill, S. and Munday, M. (1991), 'The Determinants of Inward Investment: A Welsh Analysis', *Applied Economics*, 23, 11, 1761–9.

Hill, S. and Munday, M. (1992), 'The UK Regional Distribution of Foreign Direct Investment: Analysis and Determinants', *Regional Studies*, 26, 6, 535–44.

Hill, S. and Munday, M. (1993), 'FDI and its Role in the Economic Development of EC Regions', paper for the European Periphery Facing the New Century Conference, Santiago, Spain, October.

Hood, N. and Young, S. (1979), *The Economics of Multinational Enterprise*, London: Longman.

Little, J. S. (1978), 'Locational Decisions of Foreign Direct Investors in the US', *New England Economic Review*, July/August, 43–63.

Luger, M. I. and Shetty, S. (1985), 'Determinants of Foreign Plant Start-Ups in the United States: Lessons for Policy-Makers in the Southeast', *Vanderbuilt Journal of Transactional Law*, 223–45.

McConnell, J. K. (1980), 'Foreign Direct Investment in the US', *Annals of the Institute of American Geography*, 70, 259–70.

McDermott, P. J. (1977), 'Overseas Investment and the Industrial Geography of the UK', *Area* 9, 200–207.

Morris, J., Munday, M. and Wilkinson, B. (1993), *Working for the Japanese*, London: Athlone.

NIERC/OEF (1993), *Regional Economic Outlook*, February, Oxford.

O'Sullivan, P. (1985), 'The Determinants and Impact of Private DFI in Host Countries', *Management International Review*, 25, 28–35.

Schoenberger, E. (1988), 'Multinational Corporations and the New International Division of Labour: A Critical Approach', *International Regional Science Review*, 11, 2, 105–19.

Taylor, N. and Thrift, N. (eds) (1982), *The Geography of Multinationals*, London: Croom Helm.

Vernon, R. (1971), *Sovereignty at Bay*, New York: Basic Books.

Watts, H. D. (1982), 'The Inter-Regional Distribution of West German Multinationals in the UK', in M. Taylor and N. Thrift (eds), *The Geography of Multinationals*, London: Croom Helm.

Woodward, D. P. (1992), 'Locational Determinants of Japanese Manufacturing Start-ups in the United States', *Southern Economic Journal*, 58, 690–708.

Yannopoulos, G. N. and Dunning, J. H. (1976), 'Multinational Enterprise and Regional Development: An Explanatory Paper', *Regional Studies*, 10, 389–99.

APPENDICES

Appendix 5A   Relative regional performance, new jobs and projects

Jobs

	1982	83	84	85	86	87	88	89	90	91
North	1.201	1.383	3.687	1.570	1.997	3.328	1.639	3.070	2.113	2.513
Yorks/Humber	0.140	0.267	0.057	1.071	0.120	0.661	0.866	0.248	1.106	0.648
E Midlands	1.422	0.903	0.389	0.435	0.501	0.310	0.653	1.943	0.450	0.484
South East	0.402	0.536	0.289	0.387	0.356	0.340	0.253	0.189	0.062	0.219
South West	2.057	0.408	0.743	0.690	0.958	0.368	0.253	0.800	0.282	0.433
W Midlands	0.123	0.848	0.665	2.196	3.003	1.559	1.592	2.053	1.817	1.279
North West	1.309	0.422	0.402	0.841	0.818	0.607	0.649	0.811	0.643	0.778
Wales	2.394	3.268	3.642	2.333	3.573	4.881	5.571	2.804	2.286	6.500
Scotland	2.786	3.709	3.783	2.208	1.342	2.048	2.494	1.740	4.290	1.813

Projects

	1982	83	84	85	86	87	88	89	90	91
North	2.272	1.730	1.923	1.444	1.840	1.975	1.336	2.968	2.666	1.856
Yorks/Humber	0.639	0.516	0.275	0.532	0.406	0.886	0.841	0.429	0.909	0.756
E Midlands	1.483	0.769	0.536	0.747	0.655	0.500	0.780	0.496	0.640	0.291
South East	0.526	0.694	0.612	0.626	0.490	0.463	0.366	0.190	0.056	0.336
South West	0.760	0.543	0.629	0.568	0.494	0.479	0.199	0.327	0.114	0.221
W Midlands	0.084	0.612	0.502	1.871	2.455	1.997	2.262	2.998	2.341	1.607
North West	0.965	0.874	1.170	0.729	0.964	0.859	0.835	1.506	1.465	1.969
Wales	3.072	3.192	3.190	3.054	3.594	4.667	3.926	3.037	4.726	4.864
Scotland	2.349	2.359	2.638	1.780	1.247	1.145	2.014	1.229	1.397	1.012

Notes:

1. Relative regional performance =

$$RA = \frac{\text{regional share of UK new inward investment projects (jobs)}}{\text{regional share of UK employement}}$$

2. South East includes East Anglia.

Source: derived from Invest in Britain Bureau.

Appendix 5B   Relative regional manufacturing earnings

	1981	1982	1983	1984	1985	1986	1987	1988	1989	1990
North	1.138	1.185	1.184	1.175	1.158	1.117	1.117	1.079	1.148	1.133
Yorks/Humber	0.957	0.987	0.978	0.987	0.989	1.002	1.010	0.979	0.962	0.947
E Midlands	0.934	0.958	0.950	0.952	0.925	0.945	0.960	0.942	0.979	0.951
South East	1.018	0.960	0.965	0.963	0.994	0.998	0.987	1.015	1.019	1.029
South West	1.028	1.049	1.055	1.052	1.071	1.078	1.076	1.052	1.033	1.009
W Midlands	0.922	0.920	0.915	0.902	0.906	0.916	0.928	0.955	0.950	0.967
North West	1.027	1.061	1.065	1.078	1.060	1.020	1.030	1.008	0.999	1.007
Wales	1.068	1.086	1.080	1.133	1.066	1.080	1.046	1.041	1.015	0.994
Scotland	1.015	1.046	1.058	1.052	1.006	1.019	1.010	0.997	0.976	0.992

Note:

Relative Manufacturing Earnings =

$$RME = \frac{\text{Average manufacturing earnings in region}}{\text{Average manufacturing earnings in UK}}$$

Source: derived from NIERC/OEF regional database.

Appendix 5C   Financial incentives: regional preferential assistance index (UK = 1.000)

	1981	1982	1983	1984	1985	1986	1987	1988	1989	1990
North	3.889	3.326	3.905	3.934	3.241	3.633	3.843	4.324	4.389	3.439
Yorks/Humber	0.822	0.669	0.649	0.823	0.732	0.666	0.825	0.975	0.735	0.686
E Midlands	0.145	0.215	0.389	0.263	0.209	0.210	0.236	0.202	0.249	0.157
South East	0.000	0.000	0.000	0.000	0.000	0.000	0.000	0.000	0.000	0.000
South West	0.237	0.245	0.253	0.310	0.281	0.408	0.356	0.311	0.255	0.227
W Midlands	0.000	0.000	0.000	0.000	0.127	0.151	0.361	0.456	0.399	0.385
North West	1.741	1.183	1.435	1.471	1.376	1.581	1.338	1.217	1.251	1.062
Wales	5.197	4.558	4.284	5.296	5.677	4.755	5.880	5.519	5.536	6.027
Scotland	2.869	4.294	3.816	3.152	3.718	3.611	3.124	2.789	3.038	3.621

Note:

Regional Preferential Assistance Index =

$$RPA = \frac{\text{Region's share of UK Regional Preferential Assistance}}{\text{Region's share of UK employment}}$$

Source: Regional Trends, various.

Appendix 5D   Infrastructure index: relative shares of UK trunk road spending (UK = 1.000)

	1981	1982	1983	1984	1985	1986	1987	1988	1989	1990
North	1.050	0.874	0.449	0.443	0.306	0.417	1.134	0.895	1.044	0.722
Yorks/Humber	0.755	0.550	0.570	0.409	0.355	0.619	0.733	0.500	0.322	0.311
E Midlands	0.582	0.435	0.521	0.929	0.838	0.718	0.672	1.108	1.082	1.405
South East	1.098	1.153	1.066	1.138	1.203	0.942	0.863	0.652	0.880	1.104
South West	0.587	0.700	0.960	0.675	0.579	0.926	1.441	1.430	1.029	0.974
W Midlands	0.622	0.728	0.871	1.437	1.517	1.473	0.956	1.846	2.007	1.050
North West	0.920	0.731	0.619	0.413	0.340	0.508	0.469	0.712	0.495	0.560
Wales	2.622	2.976	3.780	2.420	2.118	2.919	3.189	2.944	2.012	2.036
Scotland	1.139	1.206	1.123	1.198	1.354	1.421	1.354	1.094	1.106	1.048

Note:

1. Relative Infrastructure Spending Index =

$$INF = \frac{\text{Region's share of UK spending new/improved trunk roads}}{\text{Region's share of UK employment}}$$

2. Because of data inconsistencies and revisions several of the elements of this table are estimates.

Source: Transport Statistics, Regional Trends, various.

6 Extensions and Applications of the Model

6.1 INTRODUCTION

Previous chapters have considered in some detail the nature of the distribution of new inward investment in Britain over the past decade, together with the economic influences on that distribution, with the conclusion that regional aid, relative earnings and infrastructure spending have been primary determinants. The purpose of this chapter is to consider a range of extensions and applications to this basic model that enrich an empirical and theoretical understanding of the regional location decisions of the inward investor over the recent past.

Empirical analysis has so far sought to explain the distribution of new inward investment across nine regions of Britain over ten years, with the difficulties of unequal regional size overcome through a policy of standardisation, that is, of adjusting both dependent (inward investment performance) and independent (regional aid, relative earnings and infrastructure spending) variables for regional employment. Whilst the empirical results are both theoretically valid and statistically significant, the relative performance approach does not make for ease of interpretation or policy guidance. Hence this chapter will proceed by considering the absolute level of inward investment (in terms of projects and jobs) in relation to the absolute level of the independent variables by region. Then the chapter will consider the stability of the relationship between levels of inward investment and other variables by re-estimation through time, that is estimating a separate relationship between the level of inward investment across regions and the independent variables for each year. Such analysis should reveal whether different economic influences affect different regions in different ways, and whether the influence of each on the distribution of inward investment has changed over time.

This re-estimation procedure will then be repeated for the relative shares model, that is, considering both whether the model can explain variations in the relative share of a particular region over time, and whether the impact of each variable on the distribution of inward investment between regions has remained stable over time. One obvious regional characteristic that has received scant attention in this analysis has been the existence and activities of public agencies whose role includes the attraction of new inward investment. The Invest in Britain Bureau is charged with attracting new inward investment to Britain as a whole, whilst as noted in Chapter 4, local authorities have been very active in pursuit of the new investor. However, to date only Wales and Scotland have had 'fully-fledged' development agencies devoting substantial resources to marketing the international attractions of their regions (WDA, Annual Reports, various; Locate in Scotland, Reviews, various). Hence a subsequent section of this chapter will examine whether the distribution of inward investment in the Celtic (Wales plus Scotland) region is affected by the identified economic characteristics in some manner that is discernibly different from English regions. Such an analysis should identify when there is an inward investment affect that can be directly attributed to Development Agency influence, notwithstanding the interpretational difficulties that occur if their major impact is on the level of previously independent variables. For example if Locate in Scotland has a positive effect on the Scottish level and share of regional aid, it will have effects (via the general model) on the level and share of new inward investment in Scotland.

6.2   THE LEVEL OF INWARD INVESTMENT BY REGIONS

For a variety of reasons (discussed at length in Chapter 5 but including the very disparate size of regions), the empirical analysis contained in this volume has been conducted in terms of relative regional performance. However, as noted above, this leads to some interpretational problems including difficult to disentangle conditional statements such as 'evidence shows that an increase in the relative regional share of infrastructure spending can be associated with an increase in relative regional inward investment performance in terms of new projects and jobs'. It would be far simpler to be able to say that an extra £1m of new road spending was likely to lead to another 300 inward investment jobs. Unfortunately there are substantial empirical hurdles in the way of such simplicity. Before considering these difficulties it is worth noting that Hill and Munday (1991) related the level of new capital inward investment into one region (Wales) to relative (to the UK) earnings, the rate of output growth and the absolute level of regional preferential assistance, implying that a £1m increase in preferential aid this year could be associated with a £1.83m increase in planned overseas investment next year.

Data deficiencies prevent the replication of this analysis across or between UK regions, because of the absence of planned capital expenditure figures. The most consistent data available on new inward regional investment remain the IBB data on new projects and anticipated jobs discussed at length in Chapter 3. The analysis then proceeded by examining the relationship between the absolute level of new jobs and projects by region and the absolute levels of regional aid and infrastructure spending (on new roads) together with relative regional manufacturing earnings for each region. Notice that this restricts the number of observations to just ten per region or per estimated equation, thence making it much more difficult for the estimation procedure to pick up statistically significant results. In addition, earlier chapters have made it clear that variations between regions for both the dependent and independent variables are much greater than variations for a particular region over time. As an extreme example, regional aid to the South East remained constant (at zero) throughout the period (decade to 1991).

Table 6.1 sets out the statistically significant results of this procedure, that is, the estimation of a linear equation between the number of new projects/associated jobs and the levels of preferential assistance and new road spending, as well as relative regional manufacturing earnings. An equation was estimated for each region, using 1982–91 values of the dependent variable (new inward investment projects/jobs) and corresponding previous year values for the independent variables (that is, 1981/90). Table 6.1 arbitrarily defining significant as having explained over 50 per cent of observed variation in the level of inward jobs and projects (or $R^2 > 0.50$).

With inward investment new jobs, the equations were significant only for the West Midlands and South East. For the West Midlands, an extra £1m (in 1985 £s) of spending on regional aid was associated with another 140 new jobs from foreign direct investment whilst the same extra amount on new roads was associated with another 34 jobs. For both the West Midlands and South East an increase in relative wages could be expected to reduce new inward investment jobs substantially. Equations 3–6 reveal significant associations between new projects and the independent variables for four regions. In each of these (West Midlands, South East, North West and Wales) increases in relative earnings could be expected to reduce the flow of new inward projects (although the negative estimated coefficients were not significant for the North West and Wales), whilst increased road spending could add new inward projects in the West Midlands and North West. However, whilst increased spending on regional aid could be expected to increase the flow of new inward projects in the West Midlands, the association of the level of regional aid on new projects was negative for both the North West and Wales.

Taken together, equations 1–6 are broadly supportive of the central hypotheses, which were able to explain the flow of new projects/jobs into the West Midlands and South East especially. Evidence from the West Midlands suggests an exceptional sensitivity of new inward investment to the specified characteristics in that region. However, one obvious feature of Table 6.1 is the absence of the other seven regions for the jobs equation, and five regions for projects.

Table 6.1   Levels of inward investment by region: significant results**

Number of jobs

		Constant	*RPA*	*RME*	*INF*	R^2
1.	West Midlands	59838	139.66	–65886	34.20	0.759
	(t statistics)	(3.32)*	(2.64)*	(3.31)*	(3.41)*	
2.	South East	29956	N/A	–276656	–0.621	0.582
		(4.08)*		(3.71)*	(0.26)	

Number of projects

		Constant	*RPA*	*RME*	*INF*	R^2
3.	West Midlands	894.5	3.164	–982	0.412	0.865
		(4.00)*	(4.82)*	(3.97)*	(3.31)*	
4.	South East	802.7	N/A	–776	0.054	0.610
		(4.21)*		(4.00)*	(0.87)	
5.	North West	79.4	–0.347	–25.9	0.406	0.828
		(0.69)	(5.94)*	(0.24)	(2.65)*	
6.	Wales	219.7	–0.277	–104.7	0.202	0.803
		(2.71)*	(4.28)*	(1.36)	(1.48)	

Notes:
Number of job/projects – defined as in Table 3.6.
RPA   = spending on regional preferential assistance (1985 £m).
RME   = regional average manufacturing earnings/UK average.
INF   = regional spending on new trunk roads/improvements (1985 £m).
R^2 = proportion of total variance explained by estimated equation.
t statistic = coefficient/standard error.
N/A   = not applicable.
* significant at the 10% level.
** defined as $R^2 > 0.50$.

Notwithstanding the results above, the procedure generally failed to confirm the applicability of the model as a general explanation of variations in the level of new inward investment across individual regions through time. Given the paucity of observations and relative lack of variation for each region over time these results are not surprising. The next step was to seek to explain variations in the *levels* of inward investment new projects and jobs between regions for each year, that is could the model explain differences in the flow of new projects/jobs between regions, and was sensitivity of these flows changing over time.

Once more there are data and interpretational problems in comparing levels of inward investment with different regions. The most obvious is discussed at length in Chapter 3 – larger regions will, other things being equal, attract higher levels of new inward investment than smaller regions – hence the standardisation procedure carried out in the previous chapter. Other problems, include the restriction to just nine observations (one per region) for each year and hence each estimated equation.

Table 6.2 sets out statistically significant results from the estimation procedure. Significant is again defined as an estimated equation which 'explained' more than 50 per cent of the annual variation in levels of inward investment between regions. According to this definition the model was a significant explanation in three of the ten years for jobs and five years for projects, although it is worth noting that for four more years the jobs model 'explained' more than 40 per cent of total variation. It is also noticeable that in each case, that is, for three independent variables over each of ten years for each dependent variable ($3 \times 10 \times 2 = 60$ coefficients), the coefficient had the anticipated sign. In other words, the regional aid and infrastructure coefficient were all positive whilst the relative earnings coefficients were each negative.

In terms of statistical significance, each of the equations in Table 6.2 is dominated by regional preferential assistance, that is, it is regional aid that has been the primary influence on differences in flows of new inward investment projects and jobs into UK regions over the decade. For the earlier years (1982–4) this was followed by infrastructure spending, although by 1988 relative earnings proved to be more influential. Although the estimated jobs equations for 1987 and 1989–91 fail the 50 per cent test for explained variance, in each of these spending on regional aid was a statistically significant influence on new inward investment job levels.

Table 6.2   Levels of inward investment between regions: significant results**

Number of jobs

Year	Constant	RPA	RME	INF	R^2
7. 1983	7660	10.613	−7739	7.778	0.869
	(2.52)*	(6.36)*	(2.58)*	(3.83)*	
8. 1984	1832	29.418	−2175	9.353	0.704
	(0.22)	(3.72)*	(0.26)	(1.57)	
9. 1988	18458	36.583	−18273	9.929	0.777
	(2.97)*	(5.41)*	(2.94)*	(1.94)	

Number of projects

Year	Constant	RPA	RME	INF	R^2
10. 1982	1.448	0.048	−12.11	0.0627	0.576
	(0.39)	(2.23)*	(0.31)	(2.96)*	
11. 1983	23.61	0.0745	−21.04	0.1567	0.979
	(1.68)	(9.64)*	(1.51)	(16.65)*	
12. 1984	25.60	0.226	−28.71	0.224	0.916
	(0.61)	(5.76)*	(0.69)	(7.54)	
13. 1985	117.05	0.179	−106.7	0.224	0.781
	(1.68)	(2.23)*	(1.52)	(4.91)*	
14. 1988	314.2	0.3195	−301.29	0.132	0.671
	(3.65)*	(3.42)*	(3.50)*	(1.86)	

Notes: See Table 6.1.

In some ways this analysis of levels of inward investment by region and by year has been a disappointment, with Table 6.1 (especially) and Table 6.2 more notable for the regions/years that are missing than for their content. Yet as seen earlier this is perhaps not so surprising, since each equation has been estimated with just five or ten observations, with the anticipation that size of region would obscure the influence of other determinants of new inward investment levels. It is precisely for these reasons that the estimation procedure of the previous chapter pooled regional experiences over time and compensated for differences in regional size. This latter factor forms the basis of the next section. If the model and estimation procedure is not sufficient to fully explain variations in the level of new inward investment between regions and over time, is it better able to explain annual or regional variations in relative shares of new inward investment? In other words, can the model explain variations in each region's share of new inward investment over time, and is it sufficient to explain the distribution of new inward investment between regions in individual years? Affirmative answers to these questions would enable conclusions to be drawn about the relative influence of each variable across regions and over time.

6.3   RELATIVE SHARES OF INWARD INVESTMENT

Once more the objective was to relate the relative inward investment performance index (defined in Table 3.7) to the defined independent variables reflecting regional aid, relative manufacturing earnings and infrastructure spending with the former and latter defined as UK shares relative to shares of the UK workforce. However, in contrast to the previous chapter, estimation was now conducted for each region separately, that is, could the model explain variations in a particular regions relative inward investment success in terms of these independent variables. Note once again that this restricted the number of observations to just ten per region or estimated equation. Table 6.3 lists significant results with significant again rather arbitrarily defined as explaining over half of observed variance in the dependent variable. Despite the adjustment for regional size, Table 6.3 is a reasonable reflection of Table 6.1 with, if anything, slightly less significant results, with the South East dropping out of the jobs equation, (since R^2 at 0.451 was less than the defined standard), and Wales dropping out of the projects equation. Hence, the model was able to explain variations in a region's relative inward investment performance for just one region in terms of jobs and three regions in terms of projects. Once again it is worth recalling the caveats – that estimation is restricted to just ten observations per regions, and that regional variation in the defined parameters (both dependent and independent variables) is substantially lower than variation between regions.

Table 6.3 does show relative manufacturing earnings as a consistently dominant influence on regional variations in inward investment performance followed by variations in infrastructure spending and regional aid.

The final stage of this analysis was to examine whether the relative shares approach could explain the relative distribution of inward investment in terms of projects and jobs for individual

Table 6.3 Relative levels of inward investment by region: significant results

Relative number of jobs (RJS)

	Constant	RPA	RME	INF	R^2
15. West Midlands	29.37	3.177	−31.99	0.984	0.627
(t statistics)	(2.10)*	(1.58)	(2.11)*	(2.07)*	

Relative number of projects (RPS)

	Constant	RPA	RME	INF	R^2
16. West Midlands	29.02	5.450	−31.74	0.862	0.908
	(3.60)*	(4.70)*	(3.64)*	(3.15)*	
17. South East	4.260	N/A	−4.448	0.595	0.739
	(2.75)*		(3.05)*	(2.74)*	
18. North West	9.635	−1.056	−6.981	0.294	0.529
	(2.74)*	(2.19)*	(2.02)*	(0.53)	

Notes:
Relative number of job/projects, defined as in Table 3.7.
RPA = regional share of UK preferential aid/regional share of UK employment.
RME = average regional earnings manufacturing/UK average.
INF = regional share of new road spending/regional share of UK employment.
See also Table 6.1.

years, and if so whether the sensitivity of the distribution to each of the independent variables was stable over time. Recall for Table 6.2 that this procedure had been less than a complete success in terms of the distribution of the *level* of new inward investment between regions over time, although with some weak evidence that the sensitivity of that distribution to regional aid and relative manufacturing earnings had increased over time.

Table 6.4 lists significant results for the relative jobs distribution following the previous definition of significance whilst Table 6.5 repeats the process for the relative projects distribution. This was a much more successful process with significant results for the relative jobs distribution in five of the ten years, and for nine of the ten years for the relative project distribution.

Table 6.4   Relative distribution of inward investment jobs between regions: significant results

Relative job share

Year	Constant	RPA	RME	INF	R^2
19. 1983	8.762	0.866	−8.597	−0.013	0.914
	(3.59)*	(6.35)*	(3.54)*	(0.05)	
20. 1984	1.404	0.914	−1.322	0.021	0.856
	(0.31)	(3.78)*	(0.28)	(0.08)	
21. 1987	−1.304	0.606	1.093	0.677	0.788
	(0.22)	(2.55)*	(0.19)	(1.58)	
22. 1988	10.707	0.630	−11.096	0.853	0.987
	(7.66)*	(10.55)*	(8.00)*	(6.30)*	
23. 1991	1.164	0.754	−1.850	0.997	0.856
	(0.21)	(4.71)*	(0.35)	(1.53)	
24. full 1982–91	4.604	0.583	−4.420	0.332	0.675
	(2.80)*	(8.43)*	(2.71)*	(2.23)*	

Notes:
Variables as defined in Table 6.3.
For full model results see equation 1, Chapter 5.

According to Table 6.4, the model is a good explanation of the relative distribution of new inward investment between regions for the five years specified. It is worth noting that for the remaining five years (absent from Table 6.4) the level of explained variance only falls below 30 per cent in one year (1982), whilst regional aid was a significant explanation of the relative regional job distribution in 1990, although the level of overall explained variance was too low for 1990 to 'qualify' for Table 6.4. The table provides some overall support for the notion of a declining sensitivity of the relative job distribution to regional aid (that is, declining RPA coefficient) although note that the overall model estimate (1982–91) is rather lower than for the individual years specified, showing the 'averaging' effect of the full model estimates over ten years.

The relative distribution of inward investment projects between regions by year is estimated via the model in Table 6.5. The only year in which the level of explained variance (R^2) fell below 50 per cent was 1989, although in 1986 it was rather close. Table 6.5 reveals a good deal about the nature and causes of the relative distribution of inward investment between regions across time. First and foremost the model generally provides a good explanation of that distribution overall, although with less success at deriving significance for all posited variables in each year. Taking each year individually, relative regional aid is on its own a significant explanation in seven of the ten years, followed by relative infrastructure spending in four years and relative earnings in just one year (1988), although of course each is significant when the ten years data are pooled together. According to Table 6.5, the sensitivity of relative regional project success to regional aid declined in the mid 1980s before increasing to the end of the decade. Overall the relative distribution was less sensitive to road spending in the later years under study than it had been earlier. The influence of relative manufacturing earnings on the relative distribution of projects between regions remains difficult to capture in a single year but clear enough when observations of the regional distribution of new projects are pooled over time.

Table 6.5   Relative distribution of inward investment projects between regions: significant results

Year	Constant	RPA	RME	INF	R^2
25. 1982	2.237	0.534	−1.698	−0.051	0.725
	(0.54)	(2.41)*	(0.40)	(0.10)	
26. 1983	1.429	0.404	−1.216	0.408	0.977
	(1.51)	(7.62)*	(1.29)	(4.14)*	
27. 1984	1.172	0.508	−0.997	0.267	0.940
	(0.062)	(5.08)*	(0.52)	(2.36)*	
28. 1985	3.320	0.361	−3.206	0.636	0.857
	(0.97)	(2.12)*	(0.95)	(2.26)*	
29. 1986	−1.908	0.201	1.926	0.995	0.502
	(0.30)	(0.81)	(0.32)	(1.40)	
30. 1987	−0.861	0.282	0.619	1.088	0.694
	(0.15)	(1.17)	(0.11)	(2.52)*	
31. 1988	12.342	0.500	−12.123	0.425	0.902
	(4.55)*	(4.31)*	(4.50)*	(1.62)	
32. 1990	3.689	0.570	−4.045	0.883	0.784
	(0.73)	(3.68)*	(0.81)	(1.84)	
33. 1991	2.594	0.539	−2.473	0.378	0.529
	(0.35)	(2.52)*	(0.35)	(0.43)	
34. full 1982–91	3.470	0.456	−3.31	0.473	0.740
	(2.83)*	(8.85)*	(2.72)*	(4.26)*	

Notes: See Table 6.4.

In conclusion the model has had rather more success at explaining the distribution of relative shares of new inward investment between regions in a given year than variations in a particular regions relative inward investment performance over time, that is, that Tables 6.4 and 6.5 alongside Table 6.2 showed a more consistent influence for the explanatory variables than either Table 6.3 or 6.1. The basic hypotheses have themselves survived this theoretical and empirical ordeal – there remains convincing evidence that the regional distribution of new inward investment in Britain is positively influenced by regional aid and by new road spending, and is negatively influenced by relative manufacturing earnings.

6.4   INWARD INVESTMENT: THE CELTIC AND ENGLISH REGIONS

The success of Wales and Scotland in securing disproportionately high shares of new UK Inward Investment over the past decade was considered at length in Chapter 3, showing that the two regions occupied the first two places in the league table of inward investment success in terms of relative job shares and two out of the top three places for relative project shares (Table 3.8). Both regions have publicly funded Development Agencies part of whose responsibilities is the promotion of each region as a location for new overseas investment. The relative success of each region in these terms is emphasised in respective annual reports (Locate in Scotland Reviews, 1990–92; Welsh Development Agency, *Annual Reports*) and compared in Hill and Munday (1992). Given public spending on these development agencies, the position of the attraction of inward investment at the core of regional policy and the paucity of empirical evidence on the effectiveness of development agency efforts, (although see Arthur D. Little, 1986; Natural Audit Office, 1992), it is reasonable to enquire whether the performance of Celtic regions in attracting inward investment was significantly different from those of the English regions, or whether the underlying values of the independent variables in these two regions was sufficient to explain the relative success of Wales and Scotland in attracting new investment from overseas. Of course explaining relatively high levels of inward investment into Wales and Scotland in terms of high shares of regional aid or infrastructure spending would not itself deny a positive inward investment attracting role to either the WDA or LIS, since either or both may well be influential in securing high shares of public spending on regional aid or roads.

The analysis of the previous sections has already shown that in general the basic model was not successful in explaining variations in the level or relative shares of new inward investment over time in either Wales or Scotland in particular. Nonetheless, given the position of Wales and Scotland on the periphery of mainland Britain, the existence of their respective development agencies and their disproportionate success at attracting new inward investment projects and jobs, they can be considered worthy of special attention in any analysis of the regional distribution of inward investment in Britain.

The question of a Celtic difference in inward investment performance was approached in two ways. The first approach was to try to establish a distinct Celtic influence via the inclusion of Celtic dummy variables to point up any intercept (scale) or slope (impact) differences. The second approach was to use the general model to estimate separate equations for Celtic regions and for English regions, and then to examine any differences.

Table 6.6 shows the consequence of the first approach introducing into the general model firstly a Celtic dummy variable, and then separate Welsh and Scottish dummies. A significant coefficient for a dummy variable would imply that scale of relative inward investment in the corresponding region was different to that for Britain as a whole. The results for relative job shares attach no significance to either the Celtic or the separate Wales and Scotland dummy variables. Hence the addition of these variables adds nothing to the explanation of relative job shares and there is no evidence of a scale difference in terms of inward investment performance between Celtic and English regions.

However the results for relative project shares are rather different. The negative and significant coefficient for the Celtic dummy when regressed against relative project shares implies that Wales and Scotland may actually have attracted fewer inward investment projects in the 1982–91 period than the values of the underlying independent variables would suggest. This is confirmed by equation 39, wherein both the Wales and Scotland dummies are negative for relative project shares, and significantly different

Table 6.6   Do Celtic regions differ from English regions? I: intercept differences

Inward investment = nine regions, ten years (1982–91)

| | Celtic dummy (CD) | | | | Separate Wales/ Scotland dummies | | | |
	Eq 36 RJS		Eq 37 RPS		Eq 38 RJS		Eq 39 RPS	
Constant	4.775	(2.60)*	5.538	(4.37)*	4.923	(2.69)*	5.484	(4.31)*
RPA	0.583	(5.94)*	0.645	(9.27)*	0.662	(6.08)*	0.622	(8.19)*
RME	–4.608	(2.47)*	–5.606	(4.35)*	–5.009	(2.08)*	–5.459	(4.19)*
INF	0.345	(2.14)*	0.624	(5.62)*	0.581	(2.57)*	0.538	(3.41)*
CD	–0.083	(0.21)	–1.006	(3.76)*	–			
WD	–		–		–0.943	(1.35)	–0.691	(1.42)
SC	–		–		0.160	(0.41)	–0.978	(3.61)*
R^2	0.662		0.774		0.666		0.773	

Notes:
Variables defined as in Table 6.3, with the addition of:
CD = Celtic dummy,   = 1 if Wales or Scotland, 0 otherwise;
WD = Welsh dummy,   = 1 for Wales, 0 otherwise;
SD = Scottish dummy = 1 for Scotland, 0 otherwise.

from zero for Scotland. Hence, this limited evidence suggests that Scotland in particular received less inward investment projects (but not less jobs) than economic conditions would imply, that is, that Scotland received fewer (but, in terms of jobs, larger) projects than could have been anticipated from the basic model. It certainly remains unclear why project distribution should be significantly influenced by the inclusion of Celtic dummies whilst job distribution is not.

Some clues may be gained from Table 6.7 which sets out the estimated equations to test whether each of the independent variables had a differential impact on Celtic and English regions. Table 6.7 shows that for relative job shares, none of the independent variables had an impact on Celtic regions that was significantly different than for all British regions together, whilst for relative project shares only the relative earnings variable had a

Table 6.7   Do Celtic regions differ from English regions? II: slope differences

Celtic dummy, 1982–91				
	Eq 40 *RJS*		*Eq 41* *RPS*	
Constant	4.845	(2.45)*	4.817	(3.53)*
RPA	0.652	(5.56)*	0.624	(7.69)*
CD × RPA	−0.108	(0.43)	0.132	(0.75)
RME	−4.924	(2.46)*	−4.999	(3.61)*
CD × RME	0.555	(0.70)	−0.997	(1.82)*
INF	0.583	(2.21)*	0.774	(4.25)*
CD × INF	−0.326	(0.83)	−0.332	(1.22)
R^2	0.662		0.772	

Note: For definition of variables see Table 6.6.

significantly different impact on Celtic regions. The significant coefficient for the Celtic dummy earnings variables suggests that relative manufacturing earnings had a slightly greater impact on relative project shares in Wales and Scotland than for Britain as a whole.

This greater sensitivity of relative project shares in Celtic regions to relative manufacturing earnings may go some way to explaining the results of the previous set of equations, that is, that Celtic regions had perhaps underperformed in terms of project shares compared to their English counterparts, since relative manufacturing earnings in Wales and Scotland have been generally slightly above the UK average over the period (see Chapter 4).

The final approach adopted was to estimate the relative new inward investment jobs and project shares equations separately for Wales and Scotland and for English regions. In terms of jobs shares Table 6.8 shows that the results with pooled observations for Wales and Scotland were generally not significant, whilst removing Wales and Scotland (which together account for a rela-

Table 6.8   Separately estimated equations, Celtic and English regions

	Eq 42 Relative job shares Celtic	Eq 43 Relative job shares English	Eq 44 Relative project shares Celtic	Eq 45 Relative project shares English
Constant	9.896 (1.10)	4.144 (2.48)*	-0.835 (0.15)	5.602 (4.41)*
RPA	0.523 (1.47)	0.623 (6.47)*	0.780 (3.66)*	0.657 (8.98)
RME	–9.416 (1.04)	–4.219 (2.49)*	–0.348 (0.06)	–5.788 (4.49)*
INF	0.405 (0.79)	0.600 (2.87)*	0.276 (0.89)	0.755 (4.75)*
R^2	0.153	0.452	0.634	0.599

Notes:
Celtic = Wales plus Scotland.
Variables as defined in Table 6.3.
* = Significant at at least the 10 per cent level.

tively high proportion of recent inward investment) weakened the significance of the estimated equation for the remaining regions. Comparing equation 43 (relative job share, English regions) with the full pooled results (equation 24 earlier) suggests that removing Wales and Scotland generally increased the sensitivity of relative job share to new road spending and reduced sensitivity to regional aid and relative earnings.

Equation 44 and 45 (related project share) are once more slightly more successful, in the sense of that both explained a substantial (greater than a half) proportion of observed variation and both contained coefficients that were significantly different from zero.

However for the Celtic pooled observations only regional aid was statistically significant, whilst eliminating Wales and Scotland from the overall pooled estimation again reduced overall exploratory power, but with an enhanced impact for each independent variable. Comparing equations 44 and 45 suggests that relative project shares for the Celtic regions were slightly more sensitive to regional aid than in the English regions.

The tentative conclusions drawn from this section must be that whilst Wales and Scotland have certainly attracted disproportionately high shares of new inward investment projects and jobs, their shares (for projects in Scotland in particular) may have been slightly less than that implied by underlying economic characteristics.

6.5   CONCLUSIONS

The objective of this chapter was to see what light refinement and extensions to the basic model could cast on the regional distribution of inward investment in Britain. Such analysis has been occasionally complex, and more often inconclusive. However, this is to a large extent inevitable – seeking to disaggregate overall results to particular regions or time periods necessarily makes it more difficult to draw definite conclusions. As the number of observations falls, the strength of actual relationships must increase for these relationship to be statistically detectable.

In particular this chapter sought to examine the relationship between the absolute level of new inward investment in terms of projects and jobs and that regions spending on regional aid and new road infrastructure, as well as seeking to detect the influence of relative manufacturing earnings. This approach was very successful for the West Midlands and South East, but much less successful for other regions. Once again it proved easier to relate differences in the level of new projects to defined regional economic characteristics than differences in the number of new jobs associated with new inward investments.

Rather more success was achieved in explaining variations in relative regional success at attracting new inward investment, particularly for relative project shares in individual years. Standardisation for unequal regional size is then shown to be an essential step in the analysis of the regional distribution of inward investment.

The final section of this chapter sought to identify any differential impact of defined regional characteristics on Celtic than on English regions, on the grounds of the Celtic region's peripherality, extant development agencies, and disproportionately high shares of recent inward investment. Once more the empirical analysis was only a partial success with little evidence of any substantial difference in terms of relative job shares, but some differences emerging in terms of relative project shares.

Overall it is fair to say that attempts to refine and extend the basic model have met with only qualified success. This is hardly surprising – given the infinite set of potential influences on inward investors. The surprise lies in the consistent and persistent reappearance of a very small subset of just three variables – regional aid, new road spending and relative manufacturing earnings – as influences on the regional distribution of new inward investment.

References

Hill, S. and Munday, M. (1991), 'The Determinants of Inward Investment: A Welsh Analysis', *Applied Economics*, 23, 11, 1761–9.

Hill, S. and Munday, M. (1992), 'Scotland v Wales in the Inward Investment Game: Wales' Triple Crown?', Fraser of Allander Institute, *Quarterly Economic Commentary*, 17, 4, 52–5.

Arthur, D. Little Limited (1986), *A Survey of Foreign Firms in Wales*, Cardiff: Welsh Development Agency.

Locate in Scotland, *Reviews*, various, Glasgow: Scottish Enterprise.

National Audit Office (1992), *Creating and Safeguarding Jobs in Wales*, London: HMSO.

Welsh Development Agency, *Annual Reports*, various, Cardiff: Welsh Development Agency.

7 The Future for Inward Investment in British Regions

7.1 INTRODUCTION

The intention of this final chapter is to draw together the main threads of this book, to try and place its main arguments in a European context, and to look towards the future for regional inward investment in Britain.

This book has argued, sometimes at length, that the recent distribution of new inward investment in British regions, which has seen a major shift away from traditional manufacturing heartlands towards outlying regions, has been largely influenced by the needs of the inward investor to minimise production costs whilst securing access to adjacent national and international markets. There is nothing startling or even very useful about such a notion, which could possibly be used to justify almost any new manufacturing investment anywhere. Such ideas only became testable, and therefore a theory rather than a description, when manifested into concrete form: that is, associated with identifiable and indeed measurable variables. The specific form of the central hypothesis used and tested in this book is that the regional distribution of recent inward investment can be explained by just three quantifiable parameters:

- regional aid as measured by a regions level (and shares) of UK preferential assistance,
- relative manufacturing earnings,
- infrastructure spending proxied by spending on new trunk roads and trunk road improvements.

When faced with equally viable options the simplest has been chosen. For example, in modelling the new investors decision process, the simplest functional form was adopted for establishing empirical relationships, with the simplest possible lag structure (one period). This is not to deny the theoretical or empirical validity of other approaches, including the conditional logit model now dominating the US literature on multinational firm location. Other functional forms and estimation procedures have been used in the analysis of data presented in this book – the failure to report results merely reflects the failure of these results to offer any empirical or interpretational improvement over the current contents. What this book has shown, hopefully beyond reasonable doubt, is that a descriptive approach can be married to a reasonably analytical and empirical method in order to generate results that say something about the changing economic world in which we all live.

The next section of the final chapter will seek to place these British results into a European context, whilst the final section will speculate about the future for inward investment in Britain and its regions. Before engaging in these tasks, it is worth recalling the increasing importance of new inward investment to the UK. In 1990, over 2 400 foreign owned manufacturing enterprises in the UK employed some 775 000 people, or some 16 per cent of the total UK manufacturing workforce, generating total sales in excess of £80 billion. Total incomes for those employed by foreign owned manufacturing companies was £11.5 billion, whilst gross value added exceeded £24 billion, or 22 per cent of the UK manufacturing total. The typical employee of the foreign owned manufacturing company worked with a higher per capita level of new manufacturing capital investment, produced a higher rate of output and higher value added than their counterpart in indigenous manufacturing (figures from Regional Trends and Census of Production, PA1002). For a number of UK regions, including Wales, Scotland, Northern Ireland and the North, the importance of foreign owned manufacturing to the economy far exceeded the national average. Whilst earlier chapters sought to define the nature and importance of regional inward investment, Chapter 4 attempted to place that investment within the context of local/regional economic needs. There can be no doubt that the success of these outlying regions at attracting disproportionate shares of new inward investment has been essential for the participation of these regions in general UK economic development. That in many ways this relative success has yet to show signs of bringing prosperity levels in these regions closer to the UK average is disappointing, but begs the question of how much worse off those regions could have been without high levels of recent inward investment.

It is of course a moot point whether the relative absence of prosperity in a region is itself a potential attraction for the new inward investor. Certainly the empirical evidence of Chapter 5 showed very clearly how relative regional success at attracting recent inward investment could be closely related to the three identified economic characteristics, which are themselves positively related to a regions divergence from average UK prosperity levels. Certainly relatively high levels of regional aid/new road spending, and relatively low levels of manufacturing earnings are themselves indicators of regional disparities. It is disappointing to note that recent governments have seen fit to reduce overall spending on regional aid, and have used the recent convergence of regional unemployment rates as an opportunity to draw regional assistance away from areas where personal indicators of economic well-being point to a need for enhanced rather than reduced help.

7.2 INWARD INVESTMENT IN EUROPE

In practice of course, competition between regions for new inward investment is played upon a European rather than a British stage. It is therefore relevant to enquire about the applicability of the basic general model to the distribution of inward investment across European as well as UK regions. Whilst a full and complete analysis would properly be the subject matter for a separate book, including the resolution of some desperately difficult questions of data comparability across national boundaries, there are some preliminary indicators that suggest that the European regional distribution may well be influenced by the same sort of economic factors as the UK regional distribution. For example, recent work comparing France and the UK in terms of regional inward investment has demonstrated the importance of relative earnings and Assisted Area status to both, although in rather less formal terms than in this book (Hill and Munday, 1993). Over 40 per cent of the 140 000 jobs created or safe-guarded by foreign firms in France between 1980 and 1990 went to just four of the 22 French regions (Alsace, Lorraine, Picardy and Nord–Pas de Calais). These regions share some economic characteristics in common with regions of the UK which have attracted highest relative shares of new inward investment, including peripheral location (in national terms), substantial economic restructuring, and the availability of financial assistance to the new investor. Indeed, between 1990 and 1991 over 70 per cent of new foreign firm generated manufacturing employment in France was in areas eligible for regional assistance (Hill and Munday, 1993). Similarly the four regions identified as most successful in attracting new inward investment in France each have manufacturing earnings well below the French average (although this is a characteristic shared with a number of other French regions that have been rather less successful at attracting foreign investment).

Work by the same authors has extended the comparison between UK and French regional inward investment experiences to include those in Spain, with some indications of commonality in determinants. More formally, Bernard (1993) has conducted an empirical analysis which compared the determinants of high levels of inward investment into the best performing (relative to size) regions of the UK and Spain in terms of inward investment. This identified Wales and Catalonia as regions with the highest concentrations of new foreign manufacturing investment, and then sought to establish the relationship between the level of new inward investment in each region, and a number of independent variables suggested by the theoretical and empirical literature. In particular the level of new inward investment into Catalonia (in millions of pesetas), was related to manufacturing earnings (relative to the Spanish average) and regional Gross Domestic Product, on the grounds that the inward investor would, other things being equal, locate in the fastest growing region. An example of Bernards empirical results is given below. The logarithmic formulation is only slightly more complex than the simple linear form, and assumes that changes in the independent variables have a constant proportional effect on the dependent variable. According to this equation, which explained almost 95 per cent of the Catalonian variation in inward investment levels, a 1 per cent increase in real Catalonian earnings (relative to the Spanish average) would decrease the inflow of new FDI into Catalonia by over 4 per cent, whilst a 1 per cent growth of regional real GDP would increase the flow of new inward investment by almost 6 per cent. Thus the level of new inward investment into Catalonia was very sensitive to relative earnings and GDP growth:

Inward Investment in Catalonia, 1983–1992

$$LRFDI = -56.145 - 4.341\ LREAR + 5.680\ LRGDP$$
(t stats)   (4.27)   (3.32)   (4.52)
$R^2 = 0.945$

where
LRFDI = log of real foreign direct investment in Catalonia
LREAR = log of real relative earnings
LRGDP = log of real gross domestic product

Source: Bernard, 1993.

It is becoming clear, then, that the regional distribution of new inward investment in some EC nations is likely to reflect the same economic/commercial pressures and imperatives which have dominated the recent UK distribution. It is less clear, but certainly likely, that the EC distribution of inward investment between countries has responded to the same pressures.

7.3   THE FUTURE OF INWARD INVESTMENT

The nature of the inward investment boom into the UK in the late 1980s and early 1990s was identified in Chapter 1, although with some faltering in the recent past. Between 1990 and 1991, total foreign global investment by the US, Japan and the EC fell from $210 billion to $165 billion, whilst mulitnational investment into the EC fell from $80 billion to $68 billion, or by more then 20 per cent (OECD figures, reported by Rooks, 1993). That inward investment should fall in a recession is not surprising – the primary concern is whether this marks just a temporary decline or a turning point in the international conditions of production.

There can be little doubt that future competition for inward investment, for both the UK as a whole and for individual regions, will be at least as intense as at present, and may well be even more intense. Moreover, both the level and UK share of EC inward investment in the mid-1990s looks set to decline from the heady peaks of the late 1980s, when the UK was receiving more than a third of all foreign investment into the EC (Chapter 1). In addition to the national/international trends is the impact of specific identified influences. This book has been about the competition between UK regions for new inward investment. If the same influences on the regional distribution affect the distribution between nations, the UK can anticipate a difficult time in the international competition for future inward investment. Analysis has shown that regional aid, infrastructure spending and relative earnings are important influences. In an international arena other EC countries, including potential members of the EC from Eastern Europe, may well have a future labour cost advantage over the UK (although non-wage labour costs in the UK remain amongst the lowest in Europe). In addition successive public spending cuts in the UK have been reflected in reductions in overall spending on regional aid (Table 4.4 above), whilst spending on new roads is unlikely to be spared by future cuts. At the same time other EC countries (particularly Italy, Ireland and Spain) have devoted substantially higher per capita resources to regional aid (see Table 4.5), and have been quick to recognise the relationship between public and foreign direct investment. Indeed there is an emerging academic literature on the complementarity between public infrastructure investment and regional devlopment (see, for example, Munnell, 1990; Eberts, 1990; Eisner, 1991). Empirical evidence reviewed in these works supports the notion that US states which invest more public capital also have greater output, even after taking account of private factor endowments. However, the direction of causation remains unclear.

What is clear is that in this new age of international competition for mobile capital, development agencies and local authorities in Britain will have to increase their marketing efforts just to stand still, that is, to maintain their levels and shares of new inward investment. However, despite the redefinition of the assisted areas map, the very conditions that have encouraged new foreign manufacturing investment to drift towards the very regions that have most been in need of such investment remain in place. Moreover the recent high levels of new inward investment into regions such as Wales, Scotland and the North, will help these regions to ensure high levels of future inward investment in two ways. Firstly the high levels of capital intensity associated with recent inward investment activity has a positive influence on labour productivity hence placing downward pressure on unit labour costs. It has been argued elsewhere that the regional distribution of recent inward investment has had a marked influence on the changing pattern of unit labour costs across British regions (Hill and Keegan, 1993). At the same time there is emerging evidence that present concentrations of recent inward investment act as a magnet for future inward investment, both directly in terms of emulating success/reducing risk, and indirectly in terms of attracting new suppliers to locations adjacent to those of recent inward investors (see, for example, Munday and Roberts, 1993).

Overall then there is a mixed future for new inward investment into the UK and its regions. Whilst many of the factors that have helped the UK to become the dominant location for new inward investment into the EC remain in place, emerging competition from other regions of Europe must challenge this dominance, particularly since governments in mainland Europe appear rather more prepared to provide the resources that have been shown to be influential in support of foreign investment. However as events at Dundee (Timex) and Dijon (Hoover) have shown, international manufacturing capital retains its capacity for mobility long after it may appear fixed to the casual observer.

Inside of this mixed outlook, a clear understanding of the economic influences on the location decisions of the foreign investor remains essential to both the analyst and the policy maker. The policy implications of the results of the analysis in this book are clear – the areas, both in Britain and the rest of Europe, that will continue to attract high levels and shares of new inward investment will be those that can best offer comparative advantage in terms of regional aid, improving road infrastructure and relative manufacturing earnings. Favourable conditions for all three offer an ideal economic environment to the international producer. Favourable combinations of any two may be able to compensate for the third for particular inward investors – for example Scotland, with high levels of regional aid and road spending, has been able to overcome relatively high manufacturing earnings precisely by attracting the sorts of new inward investor for whom manufacturing earnings are least significant, that is, the capital intensive electronics producer for whom labour costs are a very low proportion of total revenue. However, favourable conditions for any less than two of these factors, as for example in the East Midlands, South East or South West, are likely to condemn these regions to persistently low levels and shares of new inward investment projects and jobs. It is in this way perhaps that the distribution of new inward investment offers some prospect of some future amelioration in the extent of regional disparities in Britain, although there is as yet scant evidence that relative success in attracting new inward investment can be speedily translated into regional prosperity.

References

Bernard, B. (1993), *A Comparison of FDI in Wales and Catalonia*, MSc dissertation, University of Wales, Cardiff.

Eberts, R. W. (1990), 'Public Infrastructure and Regional Economic Development', *Economic Review*, 26.1, 15–27.

Eisner, R. (1991), 'Infrastructure and Regional Economic Performance: Comment', *New England Economic Review*, Sept/Oct, 47–58.

Hill, S. and Keegan, J. (1993), 'Manufacturing Performance Across UK Regions', Regional Science Association, Annual Conference, Nottingham, September.

Hill, S. and Munday, M. (1993), 'FDI and its Role in the Economic Development of Peripheral EC Regions', paper presented at the European Periphery Facing the New Century Conference, Santiago, Spain, October.

Munday, M. and Roberts, A. (1993), 'The Regional Impact of Inward Investment', Regional Science Association, Annual Conference, Nottingham, September.

Munnell, A. H. (1990), 'How Does Public Infrastructure Affect Regional Economic Performance?', *New England Economic Review*, Sept./Oct., 11–32.

Select Bibliography

Bagchi-Sen, S. and Wheeler, J. O. (1989), 'A Spatial and Temporal Model of FDI in the US', *Economic Geography*, 65.2, 113–29.

Blackbourne, A. (1978), 'Multinational Enterprise and Regional Development: A Comment', *Regional Studies*, 12, 125–7.

Buckley, P. J. and Casson, M. (1976), *The Future of the Multinational Enterprise*, (2nd edn, 1991), London: Macmillan.

Business Monitor MA4 (1992), *Overseas Transactions 1990*, Newport: CSO.

Casson, M. (1986), *Multinationals and World Trade*, London: Allen & Unwin.

Caves, R. E. (1971), 'International Corporations: The Industrial Economics of Foreign Investment', *Economica*, 28, 1–27.

Caves, R. E. (1974), 'Causes of Direct Investment: Foreign Firms' Shares in Canadian and UK Manufacturing Industries', *Review of Economics and Statistics*, 56, 272–93.

Census of Production (1990), *Summary Tables PA1002*, Newport: CSO.

Coase, R. M. (1937), 'The Nature of the Firm', *Economica*, 4, 386–405.

Coughlin, C. C., Terza, J. V. and Arrundee, V. (1991), 'State Characteristics and the Location of Foreign Direct Investment Within the United States', *Review of Economics and Statistics*, 54, 440–49.

Culem, C. (1988), 'The Locational Determinants of Direct Investment among Industrialised Countries', *European Economic Review*, 32, 885–904.

Dicken, P. and Lloyd, P. (1976), 'Geographical Perspectives on US Investment in the UK', *Environment and Planning A*, 8, 685–705.

Dunning, J. H. (1976), 'Trade, Location of Economic Activity and the Multinational Enterprise: A Search for an Eclectic Approach', University of Reading Discussion Papers in International Investment and Business Studies, no. 29.

Dunning, J. H. (1979), 'Explaining Changing Patterns of International Production: In Defence of the Eclectic Theory', *Oxford Bulletin of Economics and Statistics*, 41.4, 269–95.

Dunning, J. H. (1986), *Japanese Participation in British Industry*, London: Croom Helm.

Dunning, J. H. (1991), 'The Eclectic Paradigm of International Production', Chapter 5 in C. N. Pitelis and R. Sugden (eds), *The Nature of the Transnational Firm*, London: Routledge.

Eberts, R. W. (1990), 'Public Infrastructure and Regional Economic Development', *Economic Review*, 26.1, 15–27.

Eisner, R. (1991), 'Infrastructure and Regional Economic Performance: Comment', *New England Economic Review*, Sept/Oct, 47–58.

Freidman, J., Gerlowski, D. A. and Silberman, J. (1992), 'What Attracts Foreign Multinational Corporations? Evidence of Branch Plant Location in the United States', *Journal of Regional Science*, 32.4, 403–18.

Frobel, F., Heinrichs, J. and Kreye, O. (1980), *The New International Division of Labour*, Cambridge: Cambridge University Press.

Glickman, N. and Woodward, D. (1988), 'The Location of FDI in the US: Patterns and Determinants', *International Regional Science Review*, 11.2, 137–54.

Graham, E. M. and Krugman, P. (1989), *Foreign Direct Investment in the US*, Washington: Institute of International Economics.

Grubaugh, N. (1987), 'The Determinants of Foreign Direct Investment', *Review of Economics and Statistics*, 69, 149–52.

Hill, S. and Keegan, J. (1993), *Made in Wales: Relative Manufacturing Performance*, Cardiff: CBI Wales.

Hill, S. and Morris, J. (1991), *Wales in the 1990s*, London: EIU.

Hill, S. and Munday, M. (1991), 'The Determinants of Inward Investment: A Welsh Analysis', *Applied Economics*, 23, 1761–9.

Hill, S. and Munday, M. (1992), 'The UK Regional Distribution of Foreign Direct Investment: Analysis and Determinants', *Regional Studies*, 26, 6, 535–44.

Hood, N. and Young, S. (1979), *The Economics of Multinational Enterprise*, London: Longman.

Hood, N. and Young, S. (1983), *Multinational Investment Strategies in the British Isles*, London: HMSO.

Hymer, S. (1976), *International Operations of National Firms: A Study of Foreign Direct Investment*, Cambridge, Mass.: MIT Press.

Kay, N. M. (1983), 'Multinational Enterprise: A Review Article', *Scottish Journal of Political Economy*, 30, 304–12.

Kindleberger, C. P. (1969), *American Business Abroad: Six Lectures on Direct Investment*, New Haven, Conn.: Yale University Press.

Knickerbocker, F. T. (1973), *Oligopolistic Reaction and the Multinational Enterprise*, Cambridge, Mass.: Harvard University Press.

Kojima, K. (1973), 'A Macroeconomic Approach to FDI', *Hitotsubashi Journal of Economics*, 14.1, 1–21.

Little, J. S. (1978), 'Locational Decisions of Foreign Direct Investors in the US', *New England Economic Review*, July/August, 43–63.

Luger, M. I. and Shetty, S. (1985), 'Determinants of Foreign Plant Start-Ups in the United States: Lessons for Policy-Makers in the Southeast', *Vanderbuilt Journal of Transactional Law*, 223–45.

Lunn, J. (1980), 'Determinants of US Direct Investment in the EEC', *European Economic Review*, January, 93–101.

McConnell, J. E. (1980), 'FDI in the US', *Annals of the Institute of American Geographers*, 70.2, 259–70.

McDermott, P. J. (1977), 'Overseas Investment and the Industrial Geography of the UK', *Area*, 9, 200–207.

Morris, J. (1987), 'Industrial Restructuring, Foreign Direct Investment and Uneven Developments: the Case of Wales', *Environment and Planning A*, 19, 205–44.

Morris, J., Munday, M. and Wilkinson, B. (1993), *Working for the Japanese*, London: Athlone.

Munday, M. (1990), *Japanese Manufacturing Investment in Wales*, Cardiff: University of Wales Press.

NIERC/OEF (1993), *Regional Economic Outlook*, February, Oxford.

O'Sullivan, P. (1985), 'The Determinants and Impact of Private DFI in Host Countries', *Management International Review*, 25, 28–35.

Pitelis, C. N. and Sugden, R. (eds) (1991), *The Nature of the Transnational Firm*, London: Routledge.

Scaperlanda, A. E. and Balough, R. S. (1983), 'Determinants of US Direct Investment in the EEC', *European Economic Review*, May, 381–90.

Schoenberger, E. (1988), 'Multinational Corporations and the New International Division of Labour: A Critical Approach', *International Regional Science Review*, 11.2, 105–19.

Taylor, N. and Thrift, N. (eds) (1982), *The Geography of Multinationals*, London: Croom Helm.

Vernon, R. (1971), *Sovereignty at Bay*, New York: Basic Books.

Vernon, R. (1974), 'The Location of Economic Activity', in J. H. Dunning (ed.), *Economic Analysis and the Multinational Enterprise*, London: Allen & Unwin.

Watts, H. D. (1982), 'The Inter-Regional Distribution of West German Multinationals in the UK', in M. Taylor and N. Thrift (eds), *The Geography of Multinationals*, London: Croom Helm.

Woodward, D. P. (1992), 'Locational Determinants of Japanese Manufacturing Start-ups in the United States', *Southern Economic Journal*, 58, 690–708.

Yannopoulos, G. N. and Dunning, J. H. (1976), 'Multinational Enterprise and Regional Development: An Explanatory Paper', *Regional Studies*, 10, 389–99.

Young, S. (1989), 'Scotland v. Wales in the Inward Investment Game', *Fraser of Allander Institute Quarterly Economic Commentary*, 14.3, 59–63.

Index

145